Laugh, Love, and Lift

Laugh, Love, and Lift

R. Donald Shafer

iUniverse, Inc.
Bloomington

LAUGH, LOVE, AND LIFT

iUniverse books may be ordered through booksellers or by contacting:

iUniverse
1663 Liberty Drive
Bloomington, IN 47403
www.iuniverse.com
1-800-Authors (1-800-288-4677)

ISBN: 978-1-4759-6020-4 (sc)
ISBN: 978-1-4759-6022-8 (hc)
ISBN: 978-1-4759-6021-1 (ebk)

Library of Congress Control Number: 2012921570

Printed in the United States of America

iUniverse rev. date: 11/12/2012

Contents

List of Photographs

TO MY WIFE, MARLENE!
See my tribute to her as my life long companion
and best friend!

I also want to dedicate this to our children and spouses, Bernice and Bob, Bruce and Carol, and also to our grandchildren, Bryce, Lessann, Dylan, and Maria. We have been blest with good family life!

Preface

In some ways life is a story. We take our journey as a part of a larger story and we find ourselves hearing stories, making our own stories, and then telling stories. Some stories are funny and others tragic. We all experience happy hours and moments of terror. There are stories about sunshine and storms. There are interludes of sickness and sorrow, but we all want to know the rest of the story. As author, John Eldredge wrote, "Stories shed light on our lives." To get to know someone we need to hear their stories. Here are some stories from my life. Hopefully they will enable you to laugh, love, and lift.

These stories are about a boy, a son, a brother, a friend, a lover, a husband, a father, a pastor, a bishop, a church administrator, and a grandfather. George Bernard Shaw wrote, "The man who writes about himself and his own time is the only man who writes about all people and all time." My hope is to share these stories and accounts of life as experienced over seven decades.

Introduction

Rather than record my journey through life in a chronological path, I have decided to tell stories that happened once upon a time. These stories may include familiar patterns to some, but hopefully they are stories that will interest more than this writer and people who have known me. Mostly I write to tell the stories of more than 75 years of the life of choices made by me and others.

Each person in life deals with time. Each of us has memories of times in our lives that may be meaningful or otherwise. Some write novels that are often stories of lives one wishes to tell. Others write to entertain. Studious writers document history and events. Career authors write as a livelihood. And a few write about their own journey.

The Greeks had two words to describe time. The one was "chronos" from which we have the English word chronology which is time marked by a calendar. It is clock time. The other word was "chairos" which was a special moment, serendipity, a time of grace marked by the unexpected, and a memorable time marking one's life.

The stories that follow are about both kinds of time. The readers may discern whether the times are simply events marked on a calendar or perhaps times of special grace that change one's life and the lives of others.

"There is a time for everything, and a season for every activity under heaven; a time to be born and a time to die, . . . a time to weep and a time to laugh, . . . a time to keep and a time to throw away."

Ecclesiastes 3:1-6

Chapter 1

Beginnings

"A time to be born" (Eccl. 3:2)

Most of us live with memories of what others tell us about our birth and the months that follow until we begin to make our own memories.

It was on a spring day in May, actually the 22nd day of 1936; I was the firstborn child of Raymond and Hannah Shafer. It happened at home with my paternal grandparents living in a shared house. All went well and not much is recalled about those first months before walking and talking. An uncle told my mother that her firstborn was so small he referred to me as "a child that would have made a good photograph for near east relief needs." Uncle Dent, as we knew him, often teased me about how small I was as a child. As a young adult, I was taller than him and weighed more than him.

Raymond & Hannah Shafer, Parents of Don

Samuel and Emma Shafer, Grandparents of Don

Don Shafer as an Infant

House in Rouzerville, Pennsylvania, where Don was born

My story began with pleasant memories of a little village in Pennsylvania named Rouzerville, just south east of Waynesboro. It is at the base of the Allegheny mountain range just north of the Mason-Dixon Line separating Maryland and Pennsylvania. This meant I was born in a place that was north, but almost south as well. The family doctor lived in a little village called Pen Mar, Maryland. He assisted in my delivery and was our family doctor for the first decade of my life. The doctor's office was located in his home just up the hill from where I was born at the top of the Allegheny mountain range. He would give an apple if he needed to use a needle. They were usually red delicious and I still feel rewarded when eating one of those apples. That practice improved my taste for apples but, to this day, did not help me appreciate needles injected into any part of my body. Later, after I left home, my parents would move to nearby, Gettysburg, Pennsylvania, which is a well-known historical town of the Civil War.

However, my times were peaceful. It was a blessed time to live next to my grandpa and grandma who accommodated my newly married parents for the first few years of their marriage in rented living quarters adjacent to those of my paternal grandparents. The house seemed very large to me at the time. It had a porch with a banister that ran half way round the house. This porch made a bridge for me between our living space and my grandparents. The smell of fresh baked bread and cookies would draw me often and I would be given a taste of the first from the oven. They often read me stories and entertained me with my grandma's sewing tools. There was a basket of empty spools which provided play time to build structures. These spools were passed on to our children. Grandma also had a large lap board which she used for sewing with a half circle cut out for her lap, but when placed vertical on the floor made a tunnel for me when covered with a blanket over a nearby chair. It was fun entertaining myself for hours with this hideaway.

A lawn ran all the way around three sides of the property. There was also a garden, which to me seemed immense. Facing the front of the property, the garden ran out to the road on the right side of the property. The house, lawn and garden were in a triangle with roads on two sides but one of the roads seemed a great distance from the house. There was a narrow strip of field on the south side of the house.

A grape arbor covered a walkway that ran out a long way to a place where my grandparents kept a couple of pigs. The pungent smell of their feed and their manure linger with me even now. An outhouse was located there as well.

In my experience there was always a flush toilet and bathroom in the houses we lived in as our immediate family. But I do recall using an outhouse at some of my relatives' homes and at a few churches when I was a lad. I recall being taken to a church outhouse along with a cousin by my grandmother. As she was assisting my cousin, I teased her by threatening to drop her purse in an open hole. She told me the consequences would be severe. I have always wondered what she would have done. But I decided not to drop her purse.

One of the great memories of my childhood days would be of my dad's two brothers, my uncles Russell and Ralph, who would hoist me to their shoulders and allow me to pick and eat the sweet grapes overhead from the grape arbor. They called it "wolfing the grapes." They were so sweet and my grandma made grape jelly that was even better.

I also enjoyed throwing small crab apples, fruit of a tree in the front yard. A few times there was the temptation to throw at passing vehicles, but reprimands from the house would dampen my yearning to finish my pitches. This may have inhibited my chances of becoming a major league pitcher.

The garden seemed a place of wonder. My grandparents had created recessed walkways in the garden that provided access to the different sections. They kept it well weeded. The one section despised by me was the asparagus plot. My mother prepared this veggie with milk and toast, which I detested. Therefore, one day I declared it a weed and pulled all of the growing plants. For this unacceptable exploit, there was a sound scolding. It took years before I enjoyed eating the stuff. My dad always insisted that we take something of every food on the table. If we didn't help ourselves, he would serve us, and we soon learned to never take that option. He always gave us more than we wanted!

Another memorable event in the garden was playing doctor with one of my cousins. There were some colorful leaves along the fence bordering the garden and she allowed me to generously rub her face and head. The next morning her eyes were swollen shut. Her face was puffy and she endured pain and itch. The leaves were poison ivy and it was made clear they should be avoided at all cost. Seeing my cousin suffer helped me identify those leaves the rest of my life. I received lectures about poison leaves from my parents and grandparents, which aided in my learning.

There was a hand pump on an enclosed back porch which produced clear, cool, mountain water. A small cloth bag tied to the mouth of the pump strained any debris from the pipes, and a tin cup hung by the pump handle. It was so refreshing in the summer to drink from that old battered tin cup used by any who so desired. It was a common cup and no one seemed worried about germs.

Such was the beginning of time for me as a lad.

When I was two years old my parents moved for a part of the year to Reed, Maryland. In the fall of 1938 my sister, Thelma, was born on October 9th and became part of my world.

One day, my dad went to help in a field and I tried to follow out a long lane but was soon lost. I could hear my mother calling but I decided to sit in some tall grass and nurse my disappointment in being left behind. A neighbor lady spotted me and took me to the house. Then my mother, in tears, and hugging me tightly, told me there was a possibility of falling into what she called "sink holes." It sounded like my life had been spared. My mother was so grateful to have me back she didn't punish me for running away. We moved back to Rouzerville, Pennsylvania, and my memories of childhood days playing with my sister, Thelma, are pleasant. I also enjoyed trips to the local store where they had candy and ice cream treats.

Our next move was to Chambersburg, Pennsylvania, another civil war town. It was in the spring of 1942 that my only brother, Sam, was born on March 21st. It was a blessing to have a brother. My dad had taken a job at the local Chevrolet dealer. It was a time of discovery. At one point my sister, Thelma, contracted scarlet fever. We were quarantined. This meant we had a tag placed on the front door by the health department that informed any visitors of the contagious disease that was in our residence. An older cousin, Alice Minnich, who came to help my mother, informed me the door tag meant if caught outside I would be taken to jail. My suspicion was that she just didn't want me outdoors. Well, as a young lad, it was natural to test her challenge. One day I cautiously slipped out the back door. Coming to the front of the house, a policeman on a motorcycle with a sidecar stopped at the curb. My heart almost stopped as well. I was thinking, heart pounding, that the sidecar would surely be my ride to jail. Hiding behind a large pine tree by the side of the house it was scary to watch the officer get off his cycle. He walked up on the front porch and read the sign and then left. Making a hasty retreat, pulse still pounding, my return to the house was in haste lest the policeman cart me off to the county prison! Neither my cousin nor my parents were informed of this episode.

The United States was involved in World War II in 1942. As a lad I felt the impact in the community in which we lived. The town of Chambersburg practiced "blackouts"; a time at night when all lights were to be turned off so potential German bombers could not target the area. We lived near an army depot called Letterkenny. It was a time of having nightmares about the Nazi army coming and capturing our family. The newspaper and radio had stories of the violence in Europe but it seemed very close. It was a terrifying time for a young lad.

In the spring of 1942, I started public school. There were long walks to Thaddeus Steven's elementary school. Some relatives of my mother's family, June and John Byers would come by and accompany me in the early months.

Then there was Patsy, a neighbor girl, who was one of my first playmates. Aside from my parents, she was the first person to inform me about the differences between boys and girls. We had a swing on the front porch. She told me to lie on the floor under the swing. She sat on the swing, informed me she had no panties on and invited me to see what little girls looked like! It was a strange but enlightening experience. But being only six years old, she seemed like a "weird" kid to me.

Before finishing my first year of elementary school in Chambersburg, my parents moved back to Waynesboro, Pennsylvania, early in 1943.

Chapter 2

Waynesboro

We lived on a street named Fairview Avenue. The first house we lived in was just a half block from Main Street, which intersected with Fairview Avenue at the top of a hill. It was on the east side of town on an elevation providing a view across the hills of farms beyond a greenhouse and nursery. It was a quiet little town, although it seemed like a city to me. At the time the town had two large industries, Frick Company and Landis Tool Company.

House in Waynesboro, Pennsylvania, 1942-1944

One of the major reasons for our move to Waynesboro was to assist the rebirth of a church. Pastor Samuel Wolgemuth had invited my parents to be part of opening the Fairview Avenue Brethren in Christ church that had been closed for some years. This became a central focus of our life. My grandparents were deacons. Our family did the janitorial work. I recall dusting pews and placing the hymnals in the racks. And Pastor Sam Wolgemuth was a very affirming mentor in my life.

*Sam & Grace Wolgemuth, Pastor
and Wife in Waynesboro, Pennsylvania*

There was a coal-fired furnace in the church basement. It became my chore to carry out the ashes. One cold winter day I was dumping a heavy tub of ashes. With a light snow on the pile I liked hearing the hot ashes sizzling as they rolled down the longer side of the pile. But, I slipped and I fell, careening down the rough, frozen pile of ashes. As I limped away, I saw blood on my shoes. I ended up in the doctor's office needing a tetanus shot and five stitches on my knee. It left a scar that I would carry the rest of my life.

Sometime during this decade we moved to a double house just down the street and diagonally across the street from our church, 133 Fairview Avenue. It was a double house and now my grandparents once again lived next to us. I loved this arrangement.

House in Waynesboro, Pennsylvania, 1944-1954

I recall my parents taking us on picnics and enjoying local parks. We seldom took long trips, except for annual vacations to the seashore. They took us to church on a regular basis. My observation was they loved the local pastor and church. It was just part of our life together. And, along with some peers, church was really a pleasant experience for me as a young juvenile.

My parents created a sense of anticipation, especially at Christmas time. As children we were eager to see the decorated Christmas tree and open gifts on Christmas morning. We usually would rise early and encourage, even beg, our parents to go downstairs for our gifts. Our family was not wealthy, but our parents gave us a rich heritage. We were loved and disciplined in a very enlivening family life.

Chapter 3

Siblings

In the spring of 1943, on May 23rd, just one day after my eighth birthday, my second sister, Doris, was born. Now I had two sisters and one brother. For some reason, as the oldest child I felt obligated to watch over them and give them guidance. They informed me numerous times they had no need for my oversight!

I was 14 years old when my youngest sister, Nancy, was born, also in the month of May, the fifth day. So now there were five children. Since Nancy was fourteen years younger she seemed a bit favored. But all four of us enjoyed this younger sibling.

Don's siblings, Nancy, Sam, Doris, and Thelma

I still marvel that our family of seven all lived in a half house with only one bathroom. My brother and I shared a double bed. This was before the days of queen and king sized beds. A larger bed would not have fit in the room. Our room was especially narrow since a balcony was cut into the one side. We enjoyed that feature, but it made for very small quarters. We did have one bureau and a moveable closet.

I recall my brother and I would argue about staying on each other's side of the bed. He recalls we actually strung a string down the middle to mark off our sides.

One memory was that my brother was sucking his thumb well beyond the age when most kids stop. My parents had tried a number of things to motivate him to cease but to no avail. One night our dad stopped by our bed and said if he caught my brother sucking his thumb he would slap his face really hard. Now this was a new and severe threat since our dad never struck us except for occasional spankings. My brother laid there in the dark and then asked me if I thought dad would really do it. I think we both believed dad would not carry out such a threat. But I recall telling him, I was sure he would slap him so hard it would make him ugly the rest of his life. I thought it was my job, as the older brother, to enforce the gravity of my father's rules! It worked since my brother's fear stopped him from continuing the practice. I think he forgave my dad, but likely always wondered about my counsel.

Even though the house looks so small years later, at the time it seemed ample and my mother would often entertain others for meals.

Pastor Sam Wolgemuth and his wife, Grace, had five children so we often visited their home. The pastor's mother, Cecelia, would often come from Lancaster County, Pennsylvania, and would read Bible stories. My siblings and I would be included along with her grandchildren. My admiration for our pastor and the joy I experienced from our pastor and local church, as a young lad, was likely a factor that would later lead me to consider the ministry as a possible vocation.

The anticipation at Christmas time was so strong that one Christmas Eve, my sister Thelma and I crawled over to an open grate that allowed warm air to heat the upstairs. We attempted a sneak preview of the tree and gifts. Our parents heard us and with a word of warning we hurriedly crept back to our beds and snuggled under the covers to wait for Christmas morning.

As a hobby, along with my younger brother, Sam, we both became interested in model trains. We built a small train town in our basement. With our dad's help we remodeled a former coal bin. We actually hung a wooden floor from the ceiling joists. We then used plywood to build the platform for our trains and village resulting in a decent layout. My brother assisted me on my paper route and we used our savings to enhance our hobby. Our train was a Lionel and we used the Plasticville models for the village. We erected our own tunnels and laid out streets and enhanced the set up with lights in the buildings along with figures of people and vehicles.

Chapter 4

Work and Ethics

During my young adolescence, my grandparents came to live on the other side of our double house. My grandfather would often take me, at the age of eight, along to mow a church cemetery just inside the Maryland state border. It was in a village called Ringgold, Maryland. He gave me the privilege of running the power mower while he would hand mow around the tomb stones. I thought I had arrived in this world. This place became a favorite spot. Often on warm summer days my grandfather would take me up on top of the hill to a small store and I had Nehi orange soda and vanilla ice cream. I can still smell and taste those refreshing moments in time.

The Ringgold cemetery was on a rather steep hill and at the base was the Ringgold Brethren in Christ church facility, called the Ringgold Meeting House. It had been closed for weekly Sunday services, but in the fall, groups of people from several churches would come and clean the church.

They then held weekend services called "love feasts." These events included long sermons, feet washing, Holy Communion (which was then called The Lord's Supper), and many gospel songs.

The sermons on Saturday prior to The Lord's Supper would be admonitions to follow the practices of the church. The preachers would also advise believers to mend any broken relationships with one another before the evening service when the communion was served. Young believers were encouraged in our church to participate in communion.

15

One irreverent side of a few boys was to see who could take the biggest swallow from the common cup that was passed. I should note that in our tradition, it was sweet grape juice not wine! The meals in the basement were most memorable. The menu always featured Lebanon bologna, chicken corn soup, apple butter, peanut butter, homemade rolls, cookies and coffee. But, as children, we could only smell the coffee, a forbidden drink for adolescents. This church building has been restored as a historical meeting house of the Brethren in Christ and is still standing as a memorial of early church life in our tradition. It still has the old oil lamps and simple furnishing including a cradle for infants.

This was also the time I decided to follow Jesus. The church would conduct what they called "revivals" usually in the fall or winter months. They would hold evening services for about two weeks with an evangelist as guest speaker. After one of those services, I recall making a decision to become a disciple of Jesus and informed my parents that night when they would often pray with us by our bedside. They relayed the information to our pastor and soon after I was invited to be baptized and join the local church at the young age of eight—a practice frowned upon by many of the churches at that time. It was a commitment I have kept, although there were needed times of renewal now and then! Like most adolescents, my faith would be challenged from time to time by what a later pastor called "happy hormones."

Also during my pre-teen years my parents had a strong belief that a busy boy would avoid times of trouble. There was strong encouragement to take jobs. During my adolescent years my dad and his two brothers had an auto body shop. They would repair autos that had been in fender benders or even worse. They would restore them to original likeness. They would also paint cars with a new sheen and their work was sought by many. My help was to sand those cars and often my fingers were worn nearly raw. The art of seeing something damaged and restored to new life was something I could apply to human relationships. But the work of sanding rusted and dented cars turned me to other ventures.

Another job was being a paperboy and it was a long route. There were over 200 customers. In those times boys not only delivered papers, but once a week collected the payment. It was truly a time of learning. Some of the obvious rich people would tip less at Christmas than some of those with fewer resources. My parents had taught me to avoid such places as taverns, but one such locale was a customer and wanted the paper delivered inside on the bar! I found out they were most friendly and the strange smell of beer and alcohol was a new experience. The tavern bartender was a generous tipper. But the fear of such haunts kept me safely away from that lifestyle.

A single lady from whom I was collecting money lived in an upstairs apartment over a barbershop. One Saturday morning I rang her door bell. She called down the stairs, "come on up sonny." Climbing the long stairs, we met at the top landing where she appeared with the money wearing only a bra and panties. Being in high school I was becoming more informed about the opposite sex. I must confess girls were beginning to be a part of my fascination. I, of course, related this exciting episode to my fellow paper carriers who didn't believe me. I described my experience, and to prove I was telling the truth, I offered to take one of them with me.

The next Saturday they all wanted to accompany me. I took only one boy with me and the lady appeared again scantily clad and he verified my story. I can still see the size of his eyeballs and hear his whispered exclamations as we descended the stairs.

After we returned to the news agency, he reported to the group of boys back at the news plant. It was such a good report that a few boys wanted to trade their routes for mine. But I kept this side benefit to myself and didn't tell anyone, especially at home. Every young boy had some experience that he had to deal with in his fantasies and make choices about in real life.

My brother, who was six years younger, would take part of the route and dragging his delivery sack in an early winter snow just before Christmas brought out really good tips. He was not happy when my dad informed him we needed to split the tips evenly. He did have the better part of town with more residents, less businesses, better tips, and less distance to walk.

In addition to the paper route, I mowed a number of lawns and did handy work for a number of neighbors. One memorable time, I was mowing a lawn just across the street from our house. As I trimmed along the sidewalk I found two quarters. In those days, it was a huge find! It was like a double pay and I was feeling really excited. I placed them in my pocket and pondered whether I should just keep these or report my find to the owner? I had learned a phrase, "finders keepers; losers weepers." I knew it was not a Scripture verse! I had been taught what was not mine should be returned to the owner. As I mowed and trimmed, the work seemed really easy that day. As I weighed my options, the morality of ownership won the day. I reported to Mrs. Good (that really was her name!) that I had found two quarters in her lawn. I held them out in my hand offering her the coins, I must say with reluctance. To my great joy, she said, "Well someone may have lost those on the way to a football game." (The school stadium was just a block away from there.) She told me to keep them!

As I bounced home, I reported my good fortune to my grandpa who was sitting on our front porch. He called me up and, as I sat beside him, he related something I never forgot. He told me early in the morning of that day he had seen Mrs. Good place those quarters in the lawn. With great surprise, I looked at him amazed at this bit of news.

I asked why she would do such a thing, and he suggested she might be testing to see if I was trustworthy. When I told him I had reported my find to Mrs. Good, and she gave them to me, he assured me that was fine, but he advised me to always be honest.

So it was no surprise when, the following summer, she entrusted me with keys to her house and paid me to watch over her property while they were away on vacation. This was one of many learning experiences that helped me mature. It was a time of grace for me.

Another neighbor lady employed me to cut down a cherry tree. As I started to cut the limbs, her husband, a local dentist, came out and told me to stop immediately. He returned inside the house leaving me in a quandary. Since I really didn't know what to do, I pondered as I climbed down the tree and decided to ask them which one was in charge. I had been taught you could not have two bosses.

Frankly, my interest was in the pay. I went to the door and Mrs. Heffner answered. I told her my dilemma. She came outside, closed the door behind her and then informed me that she was the boss and not to listen to her husband. Since she paid me, I decided to heed her advice. I was learning about women and men.

At a later time, the dentist hired me to clean his office, but never talked about the cherry tree. He did make some remarks about his wife that I perceived not to be affirmations.

My dad also made some rather uncomplimentary remarks about Mrs. Lola Heffner. I gathered that women, like her, could be problematic. My mother would often temper my dad's remarks by reminding us both that Mrs. Heffner provided me with employment and income. I was learning!

It was my first encounter of observing the dentist who was maybe just a bit *paternalistic* and his wife who was definitely a *feminist*, but in those days I had no awareness or idea what those words were all about.

Mrs. Heffner had a daughter who lived in Hagerstown, Maryland. Since she was pleased with my work, I was taken there to mow her daughter's lawn in a really nice neighborhood. Her daughter was a striking woman, single and wore very high heels and scanty clothing. I noticed numerous men coming and leaving the house. On top of that she invited me in for a glass of cold iced tea, and I enjoyed watching her serve me. I was later told she may have been a professional prostitute, a description that made me curious.

When I reported this scenario to my parents, I was told my trips there were finished! Furthermore, I had to find reasons why

I couldn't go. I tried to explain to my mother the pay was good. Of course, I did not explain how I enjoyed the scenery! But as I learned, parents do seem to have a sense of wisdom that surpasses an adolescent boy's fantasy.

During this decade of my life our family made almost weekly trips to Chambersburg, Pennsylvania, where my maternal grandma, Sarah Paxton, lived. She was not in good health. My memory is that she was mostly in a wheelchair. She lived on the wing of a house of my mother's sister, aunt Maggie and uncle Paul. My grandma Paxton was also living with her son, my uncle Jesse, and his wife, my aunt Lucille. This was a Franklin County farm just north of the city of Chambersburg and I cherished those visits.

There were six cousins who provided a great time of play and exploration. They built tunnels with hay bales in the barn and hide and seek was a great time of excitement. As time passed, I would spend usually two weeks there every summer.

My aunt Maggie would have us pull weeds in what they called "the truck patch." Or we might also shell peas or snap beans in the morning. Another chore was helping my cousin, Marie, who was about my age, with the dishes. I had enough of that at home with my sister. I would rather have been out at the barn, but her three brothers were glad to let me help her.

Then in the afternoon we were rewarded by going swimming in a creek that flowed near their farm. It was then and there I learned to swim. And there are vivid memories of dragonflies and crayfish as part of the life of the stream. Being around farm animals, my cousins provided me lessons about the "facts of life."

I also was permitted to drive an old pickup truck that had the roof cut off and a wooden bed with just a front seat for the driver and one passenger. They called it the "jitney." It was a great pleasure to use that vehicle to go out and round up the cows for milking. I did demolish a section of their nice white picket fence one day when I hit the accelerator instead of the brakes. My young cousin, Bobbie, was helpful by reaching over and shutting off the key which brought us to a sudden stop. I might add to my great relief because we were headed down hill toward a stream. And this was years before I was a legal driver.

My uncle Paul was a very understanding and patient man. He trusted me to drive his large farm tractors. He taught me to select a point, like a large tree, at the other end of the field and then keep my eye on that goal which would enable me to plow a straight furrow. It was a lesson about life that would enhance my understanding of keeping focus when I wanted to reach a fixed destination with good results behind me.

They allowed a transient or "hobo" to live in a shack he built down by the stream that flowed by their house. They also gave him food from time to time. His existence was a mystery to me and I never heard his story, but I understood the kindness of my uncle and aunt.

I also learned about corncribs, feeding cattle, baling hay, milking, filling silo, and many farm chores including cleaning out chicken houses and cow manure. When my uncle trusted me to drive the tractor hauling the manure spreader out to the fields, it was a great thrill and made the work of loading endurable.

Attendance at their local Mennonite church on Sundays was always a part of my experience when staying there. It was more austere than our home church. The men and women sat on separate sides of the church and there were no musical instruments.

At the end of my high school days, I worked for my uncle Paul one whole summer. In those days I never would have believed that many decades later I would be invited to speak at my aunt Maggie's memorial service.

In the spring of 2006, I had a call that my aunt Maggie (her actual name was Margaret Lehman, an older sister of my mother) had passed away. She had lived to reach 100 years. Now I was honored to fly east from California to Pennsylvania and speak at her memorial service. I stayed with my cousin, Marie, who is close to my age. She had an older brother Ralph still living. They had lost their oldest brother Marlin who had a heart attack. Their youngest brother Joe had died by drowning, as a result of a canoe accident.

It was an honor and privilege to reminisce and give tributes to my aunt Maggie. She had served as a kind of summer mother and mentor to me as a child and young man. My days on their farm as a boy had endowed me with wonderful memories.

Now I could give an honest report of a good woman and speak highly out of respect for a godly woman who had lived 100 years. There were a lot of family and friends present at her viewing and her memorial service. So in many ways it was like a family reunion.

Chapter 5

School

The Waynesboro elementary school was just a couple blocks south of our house, so it was a short walk even in the winters. For the next five years the Fairview Avenue elementary school experience was pleasant. During my school days in Waynesboro, I mentioned the school football stadium was just a block from our house. Thus I began an interest in sports that has stayed with me all my life.

My school days were mostly positive experiences. In those times, corporal punishment kept most of us in line. In third grade one teacher actually threw a book at a boy who was out of line. In later years she would likely have lost her job. One boy, in my class, Randolph Finney, seemed to be the prime example of a boy deserving punishment. He would brag to us about his disobedience. In elementary school he was whipped in front of the whole school assembly. When we were in junior high school, the principal whipped him in the gymnasium in front of the whole student body.

In my junior year of high school, Randolph attacked a student teacher who attempted to move him from one seat to another. The teacher asked him to move and Randolph asked him if he could make him do it. When the teacher grabbed him by the shoulder, Randolph stood up and shoved the teacher across several desks. I recall the teacher was well dressed and his cuff links were knocked off. He just got up, left the room, and there was an eerie silence, as we stared at Randolph. The principal appeared and asked Randolph if he had shoved the teacher. Randolph proudly claimed he had. The principal, who was a large and strong man whom we all feared, including Randolph, ushered him out of the classroom. This time Randolph was finally expelled and ended his years in school. Observing boys like him being punished was an effective deterrent for many. However, I was being taught at home and church that violence was not the best way to resolve problems.

The emphasis in American culture during my school days was to support the wars and persons who entered the military. Our church taught non-resistance, which was the position of the historic peace churches like the Brethren and Mennonites. It became my own conviction to register with the government as a non-resistant believer. Sometimes the phrase conscientious objector was used by those deciding against involvement in the military. Since the draft was not active during my years of eligibility for the military, I never had to do voluntary service for the government. Later, as a pastor and church administrator, I taught the Anabaptist emphasis on peace and justice but always taught tolerance for those who did not take that position.

Of course, I was eager to get a legal driver's license. My dad would allow me to drive before I took my driver's test. I recall most of those events were done in spite of my mother's protests. As soon as possible after age 16, I passed the state driver's tests and received my driver's license. To my great joy, my dad purchased a second older car that I could drive to school. I was allowed to drive on a few of my own excursions.

One weekend I took my brother, Sam, and our cousin, Joe, camping. We went out of town beside a creek on my uncle Archie's property. My uncle Archie and aunt Alice (my dad's sister) had a really nice log house nestled on a scenic property by a country creek. We set up our tent in a meadow by the stream, fished and cooked our food over an open fire. We enjoyed watching the fireflies and the sound of insects under the open skies.

Now I had been told to drive straight there and back, so we could be home in good time for Sunday morning church. But I enjoyed driving so much. So on the way back, we took a long way home, stopped at a gas station, and bought just a little gas and some potato chips. The gas purchase was so my father wouldn't notice the extra driving and the chips were our breakfast. Well, I looked down to open my chips and "wham" I smashed the front fender as the front tire jumped a low curb and I sideswiped a telephone pole. All three of us were frightened but there were no injuries. We all crawled out of the car to assess the damage. After pulling the fender away from the tire, we could drive home.

It was hard explaining to my dad what happened. I knew I had disobeyed and was trying to cover it up and now I was in big trouble. I gave him a brief report, noting that I had learned you cannot glance away even for a moment. I did not mention the extra driving or the stop at the gas station. By this time, my dad had become an auto parts salesman. What I didn't anticipate was he knew the station manager where we bought gas. The following Monday, the station manager told him about his young son's stop since he recognized the car. Moreover he was amused at me buying fifty cents worth of gas. Well, my dad began asking questions Monday evening and, sensing he knew more than I wanted to hear, I confessed my disobedience. It brought to my mind a Scripture my mother would often quote, "be sure that your sin will find you out." (Numbers 32:23) And my time had come. He paused and then said, "You will have to pay to have the car repaired." Of course he informed me how he knew about my stop.

I realized immediately my meager savings were not nearly enough. Fortunately, my uncles Russell and Ralph (my dad's two brothers) who I noted earlier worked with my dad in the auto repair business helped me out. One took me to a junkyard and we purchased a used fender. My uncles loaned me the tools and I did the manual labor. My uncles painted the fender and matched the paint of the car. My hunch was that dad knew about all this, but I was in a financial sweat for some time.

At the garage my dad and uncles would tell stories. When they painted cars they had a bottle of wine and informed me a few swallows would "cut the paint fumes." This was a practice I was not to tell my mother. I knew she would adamantly disapprove. It was one of those boyhood experiences of having adult men trust you with their secrets. It gave me a sense of growing up even though I was just a young teenager.

I had another fender bender in a parking lot while driving my mother for groceries. It was a time to learn that driving was more complicated than I had thought. It was a lesson most teenage boys learn the hard way.

In my junior year of high school, I was given a major role in the drama, *The Robe*, and played the role of Demetrius the slave. It was an exciting time and a challenge to memorize and act. This experience opened a new area of interest. I enjoyed drama then and have kept it as an option for both observation and participation.

Also I made a decision in my junior year that had major consequences. In those times, my parents and our church had made it clear to me that dancing was taboo.

However, as an officer of my class and a young man, I wanted to be accepted. Some boys dared me to ask a young woman to be my prom date. They made the dare more tempting by offering me $5.00 if I would invite her. I calculated that the young woman, Martha, was a doctor's daughter, lived in an upscale neighborhood and would probably turn me down, so I would make an easy $5.00. As it turned out, she accepted! I observed my so-called "friends" enjoying my turmoil the next number of weeks. I chose to rent a tuxedo, order a corsage and planned to attend the prom with my date. Of course my conscience was really bothering me and I was wondering how to get through this mess. So I decided to get some help from an older adult. My peers were of no assistance and only increased my guilty feelings.

I talked with the school chaplain to seek his advice since I was feeling the tension between my home teaching and my desires to be involved at school. In those days we had a Lutheran single man who taught a course on comparative religions. He also coached our drama club. As we all know, employing public school chaplains is a practice no longer acceptable, but maybe it has been a loss to our society. Anyway, the Reverend George Bitner, advised me to inform my parents. I tried to explain they wouldn't understand, but he insisted it was the right thing to do.

So I chose to tell my dad first. I told him something had happened at school and we needed to talk; he hustled me outside. I reported to him the plan to go to the junior senior prom and he asked, "Is that it?" He seemed relieved and my expectation was he would be really upset. I reflected later that he might have suspected a more serious issue, like getting a girl in trouble. But I thought it better not to inquire and he never admitted to my hunch. He asked a few questions and informed me that I had to tell my mother.

I told dad I thought he would talk with her. He insisted it was my responsibility to report my choice to her. Well, she broke into tears and informed me of her deep disappointment. But they both agreed, in spite of their obvious disapproval, to allow me to live with my choices. My dad even offered to let me drive his 1953 Pontiac, a brand new car! He inquired what time I would be home. I quickly informed them these events start late so I needed to be home much later than they normally permitted. I was told to be home by 1:00 a.m.

I still marvel at their wisdom. I should insert here that we lived all the way across town from the high school. My dad, who worked with cars, had purchased a car for me, as I indicated earlier to drive my junior year. It enhanced my popularity at school immensely. But several things happened that caused real tension between my parents and me. In my junior year I had been promoted from being a paperboy to an assistant circulation manager. I had a desk in the front office of the local *Record Herald* newspaper. I share this because on the night of the prom, the local news reporter took pictures. Since the news photographer recognized me, he insisted my date and I join a group of couples in a photo.

The next day there I was pictured and named with my date in a news article about the prom and the caption under the photo included the words, "these couples take time out from the dance." My mother was extremely upset since many church people would now know of my decision and she was absolutely humiliated.

The worst was yet to come. After the prom my buddy, Herb, and I took our young lady dates home. I could have been home in good time and all would have been at least acceptable. However, Herb suggested we drive to the mountains to see what a group of guys were doing. I told him my dad had said to be home by one o'clock in the morning or there would be big trouble. Herb asked, "What could he do?" He will only beat your butt; actually he used a stronger word. I said, "yes but it is my butt, not yours." Not wanting to appear weak, I succumbed to temptation.

What we witnessed in the mountains was a group of high school boys drinking, getting sick, and absolute chaos. We were told they had broken into a mountain cabin. My buddy and I were only spectators but it gave me a sense not to ever get into this kind of mess. The fear of being caught in an illegal scene and the knot of guilt about not getting home in time was growing in my stomach. I finally told Herb we had to go!

It was about four o'clock in the morning as I attempted to quietly sneak into the house trying to avoid squeaky floorboards. As I was half way across the front room, from the darkness came a voice I immediately recognized as my dad. With some weary sense of feelings, he said, "It's about time!" My quick response was a real gem. I replied, "Gee, dad, you should be in bed." His reply was, "We will both go to bed and deal with this in the morning." He also added another sentence that would, in the future, haunt me as a parent. He said, "If the Lord ever allows you to be a father, I want you to remember this night!" And with those words ringing in my ears and heart, we retired.

I had only a few hours of sleep and when I went down to breakfast, dad simply said, "Give me the car keys, and, glancing at his watch, said, "If you hurry you can make it to school on time on your bicycle." I was angry and devastated. I remember not wanting to talk to him for days. But later in life, I knew my parents had done well in setting boundaries and keeping their word. When I arrived at Herb's house on my bicycle, he asked. "Where is the car?" I informed him what happened, and he told me my dad was tough. I learned later in life it was tough love.

My three years of senior high school in Waynesboro were pleasant except for the incident of disobedience and consequences noted above. I took two years of Latin and a year of Spanish. I wasn't sure I would go to college, but I was encouraged to take the academic courses that would open the door in case I decided to further my education.

I had made a number of good friends and I would lose track of them for over fifty years. I had walked to school with John Reecher who lived down the street, and we were friends from grade school through high school. Another notable friend was Tom Cross, one of only three Black Americans in our school. He came from Hagerstown, Maryland to Waynesboro, Pennsylvania since it was a better school situation. This I only found out about some fifty years later. What I knew then was his skill at playing basketball. His height of 6'7" tall was an obvious asset. He assisted in giving our high school remarkable records. There was a cheerleader, Myrna Fry, who I wanted to date, but it never happened. And she had a memory about that and came to the reunion. I had also known some neighbor girls, Sandy Flory and Carolyn Trostle, who would welcome me back to a class reunion fifty-five years later. I lost track of Herb, the friend who rode with me to school and attended my one and only prom.

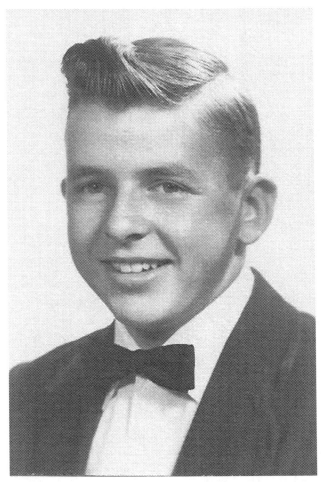

Don, High School, 1953

Chapter 6

Leaving Home

The next year was a major change in my life. We had a church sponsored school that was started in 1909 as a Bible school and missionary training institution. It is now named Messiah College. The institution had a high school, which in 1953, was called Messiah Academy in Grantham, Pennsylvania. My parents gave me the option, and with strong encouragement, to take my last year of high school there. I had mixed feelings because I was enjoying high school. I especially liked my social life and acceptance by my peers.

Another factor in the decision was that a church friend, Loren Garling, was planning to attend Messiah Academy. So in the fall of 1953 I began my first year away from home. Little did I know that, except for weekends and two summers, I was leaving as a son in my parents' home. I had a good senior year at our church school, Messiah Academy. Loren was my roommate and we both enjoyed dorm life. We made new friends and our room often served as a locale for "bull sessions." Loren had a car and we would go home on weekends since the school was near Harrisburg, Pennsylvania, less than an hour away.

In Bible class our teacher, Albert Engle, would often begin with a prayer or a song. We soon discovered our teacher would be moved to tears when we sang the song *There is Power in the Blood*. He seemed to experience grief from that gospel song. We students would sing many stanzas thus taking away his lecture time. So our motives were less than pure.

31

Life on a dormitory was very interesting and many pranks became part of our routine. One favorite was to toss water balloons from the third story at the dean of men, Alden Long, coming for his last check before bedtime, and then quickly get in bed and pretend to be asleep. He would ask who was up and when there was total silence he called us a bunch of hypocrites. We had to stifle snorts of laughter.

There was one episode that marked my life. The Dean of Students, Mr. Isaiah Harley, summoned three boys to his office. I knew the other two students. Glenn was a bishop's son. Jake was his friend and both of them were from Lancaster County, Pennsylvania—a more favored spot where our church began.

I was terrified that he may have caught me in a prank. Rehearsing in my mind all the options, I was thinking how to explain. There was a horrible fear that my parents might find out my lack of discipline. But he totally surprised me and the other two young men when we were informed that he had a sense each of us should consider a possible church vocation. He told us he believed that God could bless us in ministry. Well I had a hunch that I should possibly think about it, but my lifestyle was not communicating a track to become a potential pastor.

I will just say that the three of us ended up in church vocations. Jake Shenk became a life-long missionary in Africa. Glenn Ginder and I both became pastors and later bishops in the church. It was a moment of grace and I have always admired Mr. Harley for that day in his office. He believed in us and affirmed us as young men.

I became interested in girls and had a few dates. I was dating a junior girl, Jan, and in some ways considered her a steady date. I learned some lessons about girls near the end of my senior year in high school. I had met a girl back home, Barbara, and would write letters to her, but the girls at school were much more present so I had lost some interest. Since I had sent Barbara some letters, it seemed appropriate to send her an invitation for my graduation as a courtesy, not thinking she would come. Well her mother, unknown to me, brought her to my graduation and she had a gift for me. Unfortunately, I had another girl, Esther, hanging on my arm when we met them on campus. It was a moment of burning embarrassment for me. I recalled a country song that noted, "Trying to love two women is like a ball and chain. Sometimes the pleasure ain't worth the pain. It's a long old grind and it tires your mind." That was true!

The girl on my arm, Esther, had been with me on a class trip to Washington, DC. I had lots of fun with her and fantasized that she might one day possibly be my wife. We drew names of different girls to be with each day and evening and amazingly it seemed her name was matched with mine more frequently than the mere chance of drawing a name out of a box might happen. It was such a pleasure I thought it might be providential. I heard later she and other girls had arranged that we would be together on that trip.

My girlfriend, Jan, in the junior class, heard about it and she left me know, upon my return back to school that we were finished. I was learning more about men and women. My new girlfriend, Esther, was from Ohio. Another boy, Dave, also dated a girl, Lona, from the same area. So Dave and I made a trip that summer to Canton, Ohio. But later that summer after a number of love letters, Esther informed me, in what was then known as a "Dear John" letter that it was over. I was deeply disappointed and resolved to forget girls. It was to be a short term resolution.

Since Messiah College was on the same campus at Grantham, Pennsylvania, I decided after counsel from my parents, teachers, and pastor to attend college. Loren, my senior high roommate and friend, decided not to enroll. So in the fall of 1954, I was placed with a new roommate, Bert Carlson. He was from Chicago, Illinois, and enthralled me with tales of living in the big, windy city. He was an accomplished musician and played the organ exceptionally well. His mother would send him care packages including both sweets and diet powder since he was overweight. He would not share his sweets with me since he told me I got to go home most weekends and could get my own cookies which he thought I should share with him. I was learning his big city logic!

As a college student I decided to take the normal academic courses, a major in Bible, and enjoyed intramural sports, debate and drama. It became clear that college required more study than high school. My senior year in the academy was more like a year of fun and recreation. Now I had to apply myself, but it wasn't really difficult.

To help pay my way I got a job working in the school laundry. We called the lady in charge Mom Collins, and she was a kind of matchmaker. On my shift I worked with Norma and Jan. One day a new girl, Marlene, arrived and I was given a choice as to which girl I would like to hang sheets with outdoors. The guy carried the clothes basket laden with damp sheets and then would hang sheets with the chosen girl. I chose to hang sheets with Marlene, the Kansas girl with beautiful red hair.

Chapter 7

Love

"A time to love" (Eccl. 3:8)

Working in the college laundry, I was smitten and attracted to the redheaded girl by the name of Marlene Engle from Kansas. My roommate, Bert, was taking a home economics' course. One day he informed me there was a girl from Kansas who could bake the best apple pie he had ever tasted. He said he was planning to date her. It was Marlene. I decided I best get ahead, so I met her and asked her on a date. When Bert found out, he was livid, but agreed that all was fair in love and war. Both love and war were subjects we were supposed to be avoiding at Messiah College!

I fell deeply in love, and as I have often told people, during my first and second years in college I changed my major to Marlene! We would find ways and places to be together. Just to sit next to her in the college library was a pleasure.

Unlike some of my college male friends, I never took the risk of sneaking into the girl's dorm after hours. That seemed like a gamble I wasn't willing to take. If caught, it meant immediate expulsion. Rather, we would get away, since my dad had now restored me with the use of a car. Between classes or in the evening hours before curfew, we managed to spend quality time together!

Messiah College has a beautiful campus with a swinging bridge across the beautiful Yellow Breeches creek. There are also numerous trails through wooded areas. Many couples used these trails to have time together in what we thought were private excursions away from college life.

However, my teacher of English Literature, Miss Evelyn Poe, wrote a note on one of my exam papers. "Donald, if you would spend as much time on English literature as you do on the trails with your girlfriend, you would do better." I thought my love life was none of her business. She made it her business by giving me a very poor grade that year. Apparently from her apartment she had a view of the trails.

Marlene and Don

Marlene and I both finished our freshman year with hopes and plans for a future. Since I was still smarting from the rejection of a girl from the previous year, I was cautious but Marlene totally shocked me by refusing me the first time I tried to kiss her. Since we were spending so much time together, I recall, some months later, asking her with some fear of rejection whether we could spend our lives together. The sweet whisper in my ear of "yes!"

was most reassuring. This time she didn't refuse my attempt to kiss her!

Meeting the Engle Family

Meeting the Engle Family

Near the end of the summer of 1955, I took a trip to Kansas with Glenn Ginder, who would be my roommate my second year of college. He had also met a girl from Kansas, Joyce Decker. Our trip west was a fun adventure and we have been friends all our lives. On that trip I recall Glenn tapping the top of the car with his fingers and I thought we were developing a car problem until I suddenly hit the brakes and the tapping continued and I knew what the culprit was doing.

We both marveled at the change of scenery and topography of western states we had never seen. Kansas became increasingly flat as we approached our destination. He went to visit his girlfriend's parents and I went to Marlene's home. Later we would take our girlfriends back to college.

I met Marlene's parents and her three brothers, Fred, Cameron and Millard, still living at home. She was one of nine children. Some of her siblings I would not meet until later. Her oldest sister, Ernestine, had married a soldier away from home. Her other older sister, Mary, was a single missionary in Africa at the time and her older brother, LG (yes, those are not initials, his name on his birth certificate is LG), lived in California. I met her oldest brother, Oliver, on an adjoining farm and another brother just two years older, Delbert, in Pennsylvania.

Marlene informed me that her father would like a nice wedding, but thought a young man should ask him for her hand in marriage. I decided to accommodate her encouragement. Her father was a very direct and outspoken man. When she told him I wanted to speak with him later that evening, I overheard him almost growl, "what does he want to talk about?" I was in the bathtub in an adjoining room and the water seemed to turn cold!

In those days churches held midweek meetings on Wednesday evenings. After church on Wednesday evening, it was getting late and her three younger brothers were told to go upstairs to bed but they had stopped on the stairway to listen since they had heard Marlene tell her Dad I wanted to talk with him. He said to me, "Well what do you want? I have to get to bed." I meekly said it was private and wondered about the boys on the stairwell. He pretended he wasn't aware of them being there, but his sudden question as to their presence sent them scurrying up the stairs. I then proceeded to explain I loved their daughter and would like their blessing on our marriage which we hoped to plan the next summer. He had some questions.

One was whether Marlene would wear a prayer veiling to church. The wearing of a prayer veiling for women was a changing pattern in our church in the 1950's and 1960's. I responded that I thought she could decide that issue. Since he wanted my opinion he retorted with a familiar cliché, "Who will wear the pants in this family?" I took that as a rhetorical question since he expected me to answer for her. I responded, with a nervous laugh, that it was my intention to wear trousers. It was my attempt at humor, but his facial expression left me thinking my response was not fully appreciated.

His next question was about wedding rings. At that time our church was opposed to wearing jewelry, including wedding rings. (I heard one camp meeting preacher say the only ring you needed to prove you were married was a ring of children around the table. That seemed lame to me.) I informed her father it was a decision we would make together, but I appreciated his opinion. He was against the practice, since the church did not favor it at that time.

His final question was how would I support his daughter? I informed him I was planning on entering the ministry and while I may not be a wealthy man, I would take care of Marlene. And with that, the conversation was over as they gave us their blessing and went to bed.

Marlene's three brothers at home had their ways of testing me. Born after Marlene, Fred is two years, Cameron is five years, and Millard is thirteen years younger. The two older boys, Fred and Cameron, took me to town to get a truckload of turkey feed from a train car. It was a hot summer day and even hotter in that train car parked on a siding. They told me if I would pitch out the bags, they would load the truck. I knew they thought I was a weak city slicker. What they didn't know was that I had worked in a concrete products plant that summer and was in the best physical shape of my life. I had dumped concrete forms weighing over 200 pounds all summer. The turkey feed bags weighed only 60 pounds and I heaved them out as fast as I could. I soon had them too busy to keep up and they told me I could slow down. I was relieved but didn't tell them.

The next test was to take me water skiing behind a small boat with a seven and a half horsepower motor. You had to sit on the pier and they would get a head start with the very small boat. Anyone familiar with water skiing would know that was some feat. After several flips into the water I managed to pass the test. It wasn't until years later I discovered that water skiing behind a 90 horsepower engine was a lot easier and more pleasurable! Actually some of my friends questioned whether it was even possible to ski behind such a small water craft.

Marlene's youngest brother, Millard, was six years old that summer. He did not really like all the attention I was giving to his only sister at home and he would insist on wiggling his little butt in between us every time we tried sitting close together. One day I was out washing my dad's car I had taken on the trip. Millard was with me and he called me aside and advised me not to marry his sister. I asked why not? And he quietly informed me she had a temper and would kick him and his brothers around the farm. Well, I, of course, informed Marlene of this warning. She laughed assuring me she was not an abusive woman! She did admit she would chase her brothers out if they drug dirt in on the floor she had just cleaned. Her brother, Cameron, still tells a story that she jammed his finger when he tracked dirt on a floor she had just cleaned, but his finger is straight in spite of her attack.

One other experience that summer was meeting her grandfather, Bishop M. G. Engle, her dad's father who lived in Abilene. He had a reputation of being a very outspoken holiness preacher, a bishop in the Kansas Brethren in Christ church. He was close to 90 years old. He came out on the porch, a short but striking man with a full beard. He asked whose car it was. It was a three toned, red, grey and white Pontiac. I told him it was my father's car. He said, "Thank you." It was a response I was to hear often from him. He told Marlene to excuse him, but he wanted to learn to know me.

He asked several Bible questions which I answered. The first questions were simple, like who was the wife of Moses? I could answer his factual questions without error. Then he asked, "How do you stand on sanctification?" Marlene had prepared me for this question. I informed him a bit of my own response, but then told him it was an eradication of the "old man" a phrase found in Romans, Ephesians and Colossians[1]. A bit surprised, he asked, "Who told you about that?" I said your granddaughter. He smiled with pleasure at her and said, "Thank you."

---

[1] *Romans: 6:6, Ephesians 4:22, Colossians 3:9.*

It was an interesting visit and I would get to know him more a year later after our marriage.

Marlene Meets the Shafer Family

Meeting the Shafer Family

On one of the first visits with my family Marlene, as usual, was very affectionate. She related well to my sisters. Of course I only had one brother, Sam. He was about 13 years old at the time and Marlene made some remark about him being cute and then attempted to give him a kiss and a hug. He grabbed a nearby Montgomery pie and shoved it on her face. She handled it well and it became a family memory and story generating many laughs.

I soon discovered many people did not know about this tasty pie with a lemon tang, but a gooey filling that made a mess on Marlene's face.

For those interested in this Pennsylvania dessert, you will likely find it in any Mennonite cookbook. It was a treat of the Lancaster County Dutch people.

On another of our visits to my home it was my agenda to inform my parents of our hopes to be married in the summer of 1956. So, I asked my dad, in private, what he really thought of her. For some reason he had expressed a caution about redheads and Marlene had beautiful red hair, so I wasn't sure what he was thinking. His response to me was, "She is a strong woman." I told him, "I like a woman with some spirit!" He said, "She has a lot!" I took that as an approval.

My dad grew very fond of Marlene and, while he did not hug very many people, he always enjoyed her hugs, which she gave freely to our family and others. It was my impression that her Midwest rural, farm family culture was a bit different than our eastern, small town culture. I felt our family was emotionally close but we didn't use the physical expressions that her family obviously practiced with bold kisses and hugs. We both seemed to appreciate what we each brought to our growing relationship. My parents approved of our marriage, but wondered how we would manage to finish college and earn a living. As I reflect back, I can now understand their concern, but our love was so strong we did not see any issue about working out our future.

We had not announced our engagement, although we both were planning on a wedding after my second year in college.

Glenn and I took our girlfriends back to college for our sophomore year. Marlene had decided she didn't want to pursue college and so she took a job of housekeeping for a doctor and his family in the community of Camp Hill, Pennsylvania. We would plan to be together on her days off. The next year Marlene would plan to work, get a more lucrative job and support me to finish my education.

Incidentally, on one of my first times taking her back to work after a day off, she told me she knew a shortcut on back roads. So I followed her directions. I became really disoriented as to where we were and told her I was glad she knew the way we were going. She started to giggle and I asked, "What is funny?" She replied, "I have no idea where we are." Well I told her I heard of guys running out of gas as an excuse to be alone, but this takes the cake. I soon learned her Kansas sense of direction is all about north, south, east, and west orientation. But as anyone from Pennsylvania knows, the roads there are likely former cow paths and the compass is of no value. Thus, during all the years of our marriage this difference in understanding directions makes for interesting conversations. I'll leave it there since I don't want to impair over 56 years of marriage. She will even argue with the voice on our GPS in the car, so listening to her and the GPS makes trips more exciting. What can I say?

Chapter 8

College

Meanwhile, I was back in college. I trusted my roommate, Glenn. I would report to him when and where I was going. On one occasion I told him Marlene and I were going out, and even told him where we would park in a local cemetery near the college. He got a few of his friends and they tried to sneak up on us and take a picture of us in the car, but the flash bulbs failed and they had no evidence of us being parked. This increased my belief in the providence of God!

Some weeks later Glenn borrowed my car for a date with his girlfriend, Joyce. He awoke me from sleep at an untimely late hour, and reported he had a small accident. My car was really important to me, so I leaped out of bed, hurriedly dressed and hustled down the dorm stairs to the car. When I surveyed the damage of a broken back window and dents to the trunk, I inquired how in the world this accident occurred. Sheepishly, he reported he had parked near a grain elevator and hardware store not far from the college. He reported he noticed in the rear view mirror someone sneaking toward the car. He tried to drive off and the person threw a piece of concrete block hitting the car.

I had two reactions. One, I was shocked that a bishop's son would even park with his girlfriend. And two, when Marlene and I parked, I usually was not watching in the rear view mirror, but maybe that is enough of my reactions.

A group of guys saw us looking at the car and listened to Glenn's story. As a group of college guys, together we decided we would check out the scene of the accident. So, very late that night a group returned with Glenn and me to the site. Using flashlights, we found the piece of concrete block with paint on it from my car. We decided we would check with the owner about our findings the next day. However, we discovered the owner of the feed mill thought Glenn might be stealing chickens. He had some trouble with thieves on a previous occasion. He also informed us he was on the back porch with a shotgun and would have shot at the group of guys if we had gone near his chicken house.

So now Glenn and I had stories about each other parking with our girlfriends, and we challenged each other not to tell. Since he was a bishop's son, I knew he did not want that story spread. He told me privately he would pay for the damages and not to spread the story. But over the years we couldn't refrain from telling these episodes.

Being Glenn's roommate, I soon discovered his humanity. Since Glenn was colorblind, I must confess when he asked for my help on the color of socks I was not always his best friend.

On some weekends I would visit his home in Lancaster County, Pennsylvania, just outside the little town of Manheim. His father was a bi-vocational minister and well-known evangelist, Bishop Henry Ginder. His family welcomed me and I really enjoyed my times there. His father had a potato crop and students could earn money helping with the harvest.

As a boy I often heard his dad, the bishop, tell children stories and he warned us about using bad words. He even warned us about using the word, *gee* because it sounded like the word Jesus. That was far beyond my limits on use of slang.

Once when I was in his home his dad was assigning Glenn chores and he told Glenn and me we could clean out the cow *shit*. Now that was a word I thought was very vulgar in those days. I was in shock and inquired about it to Glenn and he looked at me and said, "Well isn't that what it is?" I guess Lancaster County farmers had a local vocabulary that was acceptable on the farm but not anywhere else.

On another weekend Glenn and I were painting the barn. I have always had a fear of heights, but he encouraged me to climb a very high ladder and paint the overhang which I believe was some twenty feet off the ground, while he cleaned the stable. Well, I thought he gave me the easier and more pleasant job, until he deliberately bumped the ladder with a wheelbarrow full of cow dung. *Dung* was the word we used in Franklin County, Pennsylvania. When Glenn hit that ladder, my heart nearly stopped and he was bent over in laughter at the bottom of the ladder. Later, I wished I had thrown some paint down on him, but I was hugging the ladder so tight I couldn't perform any other function. Such pranks we played on each other.

One fall day we were hunting pheasant and rabbit on his farm. He was in a ravine and his brother Carl and I were on either side of him. Suddenly a pheasant flew out from under a tree root and came in my direction. Glenn wheeled and shot and he hit the bird square, nearly blew half of it away, but also hit me. At first I thought I was seriously wounded. I dropped to my knees and it scared the crap out of Glenn. As it turned out, I only took one pellet since he was using duck shot in his gun, which has a lot less pellets than a rabbit shotgun shell. We laughed a lot about it later, but it was a scary experience.

My dad enjoyed deer hunting with a group of men. We discovered later the only deer meat he ever brought home was from other hunters. His friends said he saw a buck one morning and instead of leveling the gun he waved his arms and warned the deer to run because men were out trying to kill him.

I was inclined to believe the story because he couldn't even kill a duck we were to have one year for our Thanksgiving meal. My brother and I were watching dad and finally he said, "Sorry boys but the duck is looking at me and I can't cut off its head." We took over the job and he took the duck to be cleaned.

But dad loved to cook breakfast for his hunting buddies and just enjoyed getting out into the mountains. I went hunting with him once and, when the men below me on the mountain on what they called "a drive" started shooting, I heard bullets whizzing through the trees. I lay flat on the ground and prayed for safety and vowed to never go again, especially in light of my previous accident. I later traded a gun my dad had given me for golf clubs. Golfing seemed a much safer hobby! Golf was a sport I would enjoy a lot over the years and still play when the opportunity arises.

Back in college, I finished my second year, mostly trying to be with Marlene and planning our engagement and marriage the following summer. Naturally, my grades were not very good, because I was focused on time with Marlene and planning for the future.

Each summer, she went home after the school year. I really missed her. I told one of my teachers, Mr. Isaiah Harley, about my lonely summers. He also did construction work and hired me as a laborer that summer. He told me "absence makes the heart grow fonder." I had heard that remark before, but I told him, "That may be true, but presence makes the heart pound like thunder." He responded that I was hopelessly in love. Of course, he was right.

In the spring we announced our engagement. Since I was throwing horseshoes at school, we called our engagement "a ringer." Then with love letters and many phone calls over the summer of 1956, we planned our wedding for August, just before returning to college that fall.

That summer, just prior to our wedding, I worked in an auto parts store in Waynesboro, Pennsylvania. But my heart was in Kansas with my redheaded, sunflower, sweetheart. I was eager to get married and get on with our life together.

That summer my brother Sam traveled west with Marlene and worked on the Engle family farm with her younger brothers. It was quite an experience and he changed from a chubby little boy to a lanky young man even though he was only 14 years old. He learned the ways of Kansas farm boys. He recalled how Marlene's dad would say three boys together get no work done, two boys may get a little, but with one boy you may get some work done. But he left two of the boys work together that summer. Marlene's brother, Fred, tells the story of the three boys goofing off and his dad caught them. Since Fred was the oldest he was going to spank him, but Fred threw him off. So his dad said, "Well, since that won't work, you can't have the car this weekend." Fred said he had to cancel his date. All three boys were learning and growing up fast.

My brother learned many things that summer. He did grow physically and matured a lot. He was in good shape. Sam had a great summer and remained a good friend with Fred and Cameron ever after those days.

So, Marlene and I were convinced he looked great as my best man for our wedding.

Chapter 9

Marriage

I arrived in Kansas for our wedding a few days early. Marlene shared with me that her dad had changed his mind about wedding rings. He had been to his son's wedding (LG and Carole in California) and now wore a tie and seemed more relaxed.

But I knew he was a strong man who seemed a bit heavy on the male role in a marriage. Just before our wedding we made a trip with her parents to Abilene from the farm. We both wanted to know how her parents felt about us wearing wedding rings. So when her mother left us in the car with her dad, Marlene asked about the wedding rings. He surprised both of us by saying, "Ask your mother."

Well, when her mother came back Marlene asked her about us wearing rings at the wedding. Her mother, looking at her husband, said, "Well I prefer you don't wear them at church." So we purchased them in Abilene, but waited until after the wedding to put them on our hands.

Marlene and Don's Wedding, 1956

Our wedding was in the Zion Brethren in Christ church just north of Abilene, Kansas. As I said, my brother, Sam, was my best man. My college roommate, Glenn Ginder, was an attendant along with Marlene's brother, Fred. Marlene had a college friend, Betty Brumbaugh, as maid of honor. My sister, Thelma, and Glenn's girlfriend, Joyce Decker, were her bride's maids.

The Zion church had acquired a new pastor since Marlene left home. We agreed on asking the minister, who had been my only pastor from age six until I left home, to preside over our wedding. So Sam Wolgemuth was the minister who counseled us and performed the wedding ceremony. His advice was to keep reminders of Christ in our home. One of the gifts we received when we left our first pastorate was an artist's rendering of "Jesus on the Road to Emmaus" and it has hung on the wall of every home we have lived in for over fifty-six years.

A first cousin of mine, Mary Hoffman, played the organ and a number of other friends helped make our day special.

It was a very hot 30th day in August, 1956 (the same day and month my parents had been married). The event was held before there was air conditioning in the Zion church. It was so hot the candles slumped in the heat! I was sweating and I noticed the pastor's sweat dropped on our hands as he prayed and held our hands.

As we knelt for prayer, Ruth Ann Lady, a friend of Marlene's, played the "Lord's Prayer" on a violin. My brother suddenly passed out, fell on the altar rail and joined us in prayer! My uncle Russell and my dad, seeing what happened, came to his aid and assisted him out a side door. Actually it looked like they dragged him out.

We had worried about our lips being moist to kiss, but it was the saltiest and, likely, the sweatiest kiss of our romance. In the meantime, my brother was revived and was standing, white as a sheet, at the back of the church when we exited. I called him a "party pooper." The only damage was broken cuff links and perhaps his pride.

I also met Marlene's oldest sister, Ernestine, and her husband, Ira Eyster, at our wedding. They impressed me as a fine mature married couple. We would enjoy times with them later in life.

Marlene's father, who felt wedding parties at the time were not serving enough food, planned a full three course meal in the basement of the church. It was a turkey dinner with all the trimmings. We felt especially honored to have Marlene's grandfather, Bishop M. G. Engle, present who was almost 90 years old.

My uncle Paul and aunt Maggie made the trip from Pennsylvania to be there. I wrote earlier about the one summer I worked on their farm. Thus it was a fond memory and an honor to have them share in our day of marriage.

We spent our first night of married life in the Sunflower Hotel in downtown Abilene, Kansas. We had made arrangements to travel to the hotel without any of Marlene's brothers knowing about our plans. No one could predict what they might try to do as a surprise. When we arrived at the hotel, I discovered I left the keys to our locked suitcases back at her home. Her brother Fred was called and he brought the keys to us. We weren't sure what he would do since he now knew where we were lodging.

During the night we heard a ruckus in the hall and I thought Marlene's brothers were back, but it turned out to be strangers having a late party.

The next day we left traveling in our car. My parents were traveling with us in their own car with my four siblings. At the time it was a fun trip. I had to get back to college since I was president of the student body. One responsibility was to be on campus for an orientation for new students before school started in early September. Marlene and I decided we would be on our honeymoon the rest of our life!

That fall, Marlene first worked in a bank, then some months later for Blue Shield while I finished college. We were among the married students in college and lived in a specially built apartment complex for married students on campus. It was really a one-room apartment with a rollout bed and a small bathroom and kitchen. Now, happily married, I took my classes much more seriously and my grades improved markedly. However, I had a hard time proving to some of my professors I was now more disciplined in my studies.

On Thanksgiving night in 1956, we received a call that Marlene's father and mother had been in a car accident. Her mother was not seriously injured, but her dad had been thrown from the vehicle, had a broken neck, and died two weeks after the accident from a smashed spinal cord. It was a tough time.

We drove to Kansas in my father's new Pontiac car, which he loaned to us. Marlene's grandfather, M. G. Engle, who was living at Messiah Home, a retirement facility in Harrisburg, rode with us.

He made our trip quite an event. Grandpa Engle was now 90 years old. He had Parkinson's disease and was a bit shaky, but otherwise in great health. He was a spectacle of a man with a black suit, broad brim hat, wire rimmed glasses and full beard. When he drank his coffee he would accidentally spill some in the saucer and, being a thrifty man, he would then drain the saucer.

He embarrassed my new bride. We tried to hide him in a booth, but the man wanted to see people. On one occasion, he excused himself and sat in the next booth so he could see others. We joined him with his approval. I persuaded my wife, since no one knew us, to allow her grandpa to have his way. She agreed.

One day he told Marlene to tell the waitress he had two birthdays. He meant his day of physical birth and then when he was "born again" to become a follower of Christ, his second birthday. My wife sat in silence, so he told the young waitress he had two birthdays. She reached out her hand, stroked his beard and told him he reminded her of her great grandfather. It rattled him a bit, but he explained to her what he meant. She simply stroked his beard again and said "That is really nice." He blushed a bit and when she left, he informed me she hadn't taken the bait.

He was a good traveler, but in spite of my dad's car having an excellent heater, he had cold legs and feet. He explained it was poor circulation. At every stop he would explain to people he had buried two wives, one son, and we were now going to bury a second son. He told us in the car he would need to stay in Kansas and would likely not return with us.

It was a cold December day when we arrived in Kansas. There I met Marlene's older brother, LG, from California for the first time. He came out of the house in short shirt sleeves, arms akimbo, looked me up and down and asked Marlene, "So is this the guy you married?" She proudly said a strong YES! LG commented, "He might be ok." Then with a smile he invited me into his parent's home.

I was learning to know more of her family. Her oldest brother, Oliver, lived on the farm next to Marlene's home. He and his wife, Lela, had ten children. Her second sister, Mary, was a missionary in Africa and did not make it home for her father's funeral. I would meet her later in our journey.

Then there was Delbert who I had met at school. He married Twila, a girl in my senior class of high school. Marlene's three younger brothers, Fred, Cameron and Millard, were all still living at home, so this sudden loss of their father was a major crisis in their family life.

At the memorial service I witnessed Marlene's grandpa who reached into the open coffin, and patted his son on the cheek, and said, "I'll see you in heaven, LaMar!" He said it loud and with such confidence I knew his faith was real. I marveled at his confidence in God's ways as a man who outlived two wives and two sons.

Back at the house the family shared in a meal. At one point grandpa Engle asked for me and took me outside. He asked if we had room in the car to return to Pennsylvania. I assured him it was only Marlene and me so it would be fine. Then he grasped my arm and said, "Not a word inside about this, you understand?" I understood.

But my mother in law wanted to know what he said. Since he was watching me like a hawk, I discreetly told her we would talk later after he left. He really wanted to "stay and take care of business" as he put it. But neither Marlene's mother nor his other daughter in law in the area were prepared to keep him.

He returned to Pennsylvania with us and provided us many learning moments. One evening as we were traveling in the car, he suddenly shouted, "I want to die!" I recall my first thought was "Oh not now, please!" When Marlene asked why he wanted to die, he replied, "An old man like me isn't doing the world any good; I want to go home to the glory world!" We ended our trip by taking him back to Messiah Home.

We returned to Messiah College where I finished my last two years. I served as president of the student body college assembly and during those years we raised funds to establish the sign on the entrance to the college. That entrance was later changed after a bridge was built over the railroad at the other end of the campus. The older sign is still down by the old bridge over the creek that runs by the college.

Chapter 10

Marlene

I share these stories as a tribute to my wife's loyalty and steadfast love in our marriage of over 56 years.

Marlene (Engle) Shafer

In the late 1950's we were among a minority of married college students. Messiah College had built a small complex for married students. We had a really small unit, which meant our living space was also our bedroom and we had to roll up our bed every morning. Marlene was very patient about this and never once complained.

She began our marriage by working at a bank to support me. I soon discovered she was an excellent cook. And while food was much more available, when I gained about 30 pounds in our first two years of marriage it does indicate her culinary skills. Of course my lack of discipline on portions may have had some impact. She always supported my activities, attended sports and encouraged me to improve my grades.

I soon learned her gift for handling finances. We both knew our dads had handled money in their marriages, but we decided we would be better off if she paid the bills and managed our finances. At this point she was bringing home the money, so it made sense to have her handle that part of our marriage. It would last a lifetime. She had learned thrift and we left college without debt. Years later a financial advisor, Don Zook, would look at me and say, "Well Don, someone handled your finances very wisely." I knew it was Marlene and informed him she deserved the credit. Her bemused smile was always a joy to me.

Marlene is a great game player. In the early years of our marriage we played numerous table games including cards. Admittedly, we are both very competitive which made for some very interesting exchanges. It was an arena where we learned to communicate and push for our individual ways, but she had a unique way of always ending in love. I am biased, of course, but as a college student I was convinced I had chosen a woman of "noble character" and I had full confidence in her. These words came to mind from the wisdom writer. (Proverbs 31)

Marlene became the wife of an ordained minister. She lovingly supported me but would let me know she would not blindly follow current practices. We decided to start our family in 1959 so she was very pregnant at our installation and ordination in September of 1959. One of the traditions at our first pastorate was to have the wife of the pastor sit near the front. She informed me she would be sitting near the back. I could see no reason for this, but it became clear this was not a debate; it was a choice she made. I was beginning to see what my Dad meant about her being a strong woman.

Most of the people loved her and accepted her beyond my expectations. One older married woman came to me and inquired if our marriage was a happy one. I was taken aback and asked why? She told me Marlene seemed a bit *stuck up* to her. Incidentally, this woman was the mother who brought the girl who came to my high school graduation. I quickly told her that Marlene was not at all aloof to me. She gave me a look that left me know my attempt at humor was not appropriate! But this was rare.

Marlene was willing to try to accommodate most concerns. The churches in Lancaster County were still fairly conservative. So there was concern about dress styles and wearing of jewelry was not acceptable. We were told that one lady thought Marlene's blouses were a bit too revealing, so she wore a pin to close the cleavage gap. Then she was criticized for wearing jewelry. From that experience on she told me, "I'll dress as I please; you handle those issues." And so I did.

When our children were born, Marlene was an excellent mother and it seemed to bond her to the older women of the congregation who were solicitous in helping her as a younger mother.

I returned to being a seminary student. So, Marlene managed the parsonage while I was gone. She lovingly mothered our two children while keeping the house open and warm for visitors. She would host people frequently and prepared simple but delicious meals.

Marlene did not like the "fish bowl" syndrome, as it is called, when a pastor's wife is watched more closely and perhaps judged more quickly than most spouses. But she was independent enough to let most of that pass or hand it over to me since I had taken this life of being a pastor which came with some expectations for a spouse beyond many careers. She made it clear she would always love and support me but would not just accept other people's wishes that were not sensible to her.

A good example of her strength happened on one of our visits from our bishop. I had done a couple of things for which the bishop had corrected me in regard to church polity and I was trying hard to please and impress. I told my wife if I received another concern from the bishop maybe I should reconsider my calling. At the dinner table he asked if I knew anything about golf. I had just tried it and assumed he was going to reprimand me for wasting my time. My wife spoke up and asked, "Why, would you like him to teach you?" My first hunch was, "Oh there goes my job!" but to my amazement, he responded to Marlene, "Well, as a matter of fact, that is exactly what I was going to ask." I was completely surprised by this turn in the conversation. I looked at my wife and she had a grin as if to say, there, now, that was good huh?

I never ceased to admire her timing and directness that eluded me. She always seemed to have a way of being direct and getting to resolution without any equivocation.

Marlene has a sense of intuition that served me well as a young pastor. She was never jealous, but if she sensed a threat she could alert me to certain people who could become problematic. I soon learned to listen to her and check out any possibility of relationships that could hurt. She avoided publicity and yet was willing to help with projects she thought would benefit others. She shied away from offices and church politics.

She would dialogue with me, but never got into what I would call power plays. She would cooperate and do the proper things, like help the deacons' wives with practices, such as preparing communion bread, but told me privately such things she could do without. She never embarrassed me. And if I would ask for her opinions of my sermons and church decisions, a frequent response would be, "It was all right." In her own way she helped keep me humble and at the same time left me know I was the lover of her life. It was a good combination for me as a pastor.

Neither of us anticipated the invitation to become involved as a leader in our denominational church life. I thought I was not saying or doing the right things to become an obvious eligible leader in the church. I was first invited to be involved in the ministries of Christian Education, later named Congregational Life. It had to do with programs related to children, youth, and adults.

During those years Marlene liked the independence of no longer sensing the fish bowl dynamic. She liked being out of the public eye. At first I was away as much as a month at a time. She didn't like the absence of her husband and father from our two young children. Later she told me how one day doing dishes, feeling sorry for herself and, with tears rolling down her cheeks, she mused, "Well either shape up or ship out!" To my great relief she decided to shape up. And she was always a vigorous supporter of my church roles.

In the first year of my role as Director of Sunday Schools, I asked her to work for me as a secretary. This arrangement was not as good as I had expected. She did not like to respond to me as an employer. As a matter of fact, after I tried to explain to her how she should listen to me as an employer, she told me to find someone else. She came to the conclusion in her words. "You are a great lover, but a lousy boss." So we moved on. She found employment outside the home, I found others to help in support roles and we both functioned better.

Marlene always adapted to changes well. After leaving college we had lived in an apartment, and then in the Elizabethtown parsonage. During 1965-66 we lived in a borrowed house, a short time in our tent, a few weeks in my Dad's cabin and one more rented house before we moved to Nappanee, Indiana. Then six years later we moved to Upland, California. In spite of all these moves, she found jobs, chose to enjoy each situation and managed our family affairs. But best of all she excelled at loving our children and me.

She had a way of discerning my deep inclinations. When I called from Pennsylvania to her in Nappanee, Indiana, and informed her we would need to pray about an invitation I had just received to be a nominee for bishop, she quickly responded, "You sound like a kid with a new toy." She seemed to grasp my aspirations before I had fully decided what we should do. I believe I would have been sensitive to her, but she was ready to make the change even though I knew she liked her job and friends in Nappanee.

When we had a welcoming event in Upland, California, someone asked her how she would fit in the new role as a bishop's wife. Her immediate response was, "It is my job to love my husband!" Indeed she never seemed threatened by other people's expectations. She found employment at the local hospital and held that job for the next twenty years. Again I was on the road a lot and she was a fantastic mother to our two children during their elementary and high school years.

As for romance, she would do things to make me feel like a man. Once, and only once, she did the totally unexpected. I had been in Pennsylvania, and Pastor Ken Letner asked me how I handled being away so much. Well I told him Marlene always made coming home such a warm experience that I looked forward to those times. I told him she would likely meet me without anything on but a coat. His response was that I was a dreamer.

When Marlene picked me up at the airport she had on a white fur coat I had purchased for her (not real fur since we could not have afforded that), but as we drove home I soon discovered that was all she had on! Now that was exciting!

It just happened that Ken Letner came west a week later. Just before he got up to speak I leaned over and said Marlene met me at the airport with nothing on but a fur coat. He glanced back at her and she nodded yes. He turned red and then pulled himself together to make his presentation.

She had a knack of responding to any emergency and was especially strong when she was diagnosed with breast cancer. One incident might reveal her true feelings about me. The medical team had given her a drug to block memory before taking chemo treatments intravenously. I was instructed to take her home and give her medications.

We were to return to the clinic and when they asked her if she had taken the anti-nausea suppositories, I informed them I had administered them. At that point Marlene asked the nurses, "Isn't that a man's job?" They liked Marlene and laughed heartily. I think it was the memory blocking drugs, but perhaps more closer to her understanding of me.

We were told about her chances of survival and the doctor told us that my wife would likely survive. I asked how he knew, and he asked me if I was a man of faith. Well, he had me on that one. He was Jewish and he knew I was a minister, so we laughed. But he went on to say, "Your wife is healthy in many ways and she is a fighter, and I have seen such patients and I believe she will win this battle with cancer." He was right and it helped my faith increase, surely in God, but especially in my wife.

Marlene was not eager, maybe even reluctant, to get involved in my work. But on several occasions she was a very valuable resource. At pastors and spouses retreats she would respond to questions. I soon discovered pastors and spouses liked her direct and honest answers. In one retreat she gave some very explicit answers about our marriage, and a pastor leaned over and whispered in my ear, "I am learning more about you than I need to know." I was strengthened by Marlene's counsel and wisdom. Once, a spouse asked Marlene if she ever was concerned about me being alone on the road. Her response was, "I keep him happy at home and don't worry about him." Her strong love and support held me accountable across the years.

In 1992, once again we moved across the United States back to Pennsylvania. Marlene gave up her job of twenty years in the local hospital business office in California. She was very helpful in our relocation in mutually deciding on a choice of house and then a church. We both missed being so far from our family, but Marlene was resourceful in finding ways to get them east, or we would travel west.

I write later about my time at Messiah Village, but just to say here that Marlene was especially supportive when I was terminated as an employee. It was the hardest point in my career. She loved me deeply and then tried to solace me by saying it would get us back to California earlier than we had anticipated. She had a unique capacity to encourage me and others when it was needed.

So in the summer of 2000 we moved back to California and Marlene once more handled issues with zeal because it was getting us closer to our family and I was entering those times some folk call senior years.

Our first move was to Moreno Valley, California, where we lived in a large rented house. There we served as interim pastor at the Riverside Brethren in Christ Church. Marlene supported our move and affirmed me in this role. She was loved by the local church people. She could work harder than most people our children's age and on clean up days at the church would amaze younger people by her stamina.

In 2002 we both decided to have a house built, a first in our married life. Our son, Bruce, had encouraged us to look for property and build. We found an affordable plot of land, actually two and a half acres, in Pinon Hills, California, and employed a local builder. We both found real joy in this project. Some people had warned us that building a house can stress a marriage, but in our case we found it an exciting challenge that we both enjoyed. I would credit this to my wife's strength and wisdom with planning and finances. We have both enjoyed our life in Pinon Hills. I got involved in other interim pastoral roles, but in every case Marlene was consistently supportive and loving.

When we found a winter cabin in Yuma, Arizona, I saw a new side to Marlene. She became very active in crafts. Over the years she had demonstrated her ability. Our home has ceramic artifacts and other pieces from the work of her hands. But now she learned new crafts, especially iris folding cards and she would sell those and other crafts of beads or cloth and vendor them at craft fairs. She also enjoyed playing games with others. She amazed me by becoming a good shuffleboard player and even tried the pool table at which she did very well. She can be very independent and we both have enjoyed finding and making new friends. She has a way of connecting with strangers that far excels my ability. So we eagerly embrace this part of our life together.

One other surprise came after we had made several cross-country trips. In the summer of 2010 we visited her cousin and learned of a vegetarian life style. Marlene embraced this and has creatively prepared meals, which we both believe will enhance our health. We have both embraced a lifestyle of exercise using "Silver Sneakers" provided by health insurance carriers as well as our regimen of walking. I have discovered Marlene walks faster and so she and a neighbor lady walk faster and further than me, but I am glad to see this strong woman enhance our life together as snowbirds in Yuma, Arizona. It is beyond anything I ever imagined. Again I affirm the Biblical chapter of Proverbs 31 as an apt description of my woman, my lover, my wife.

Chapter 11

Pastor

A most memorable event occurred during my senior year in college when I received an invitation to assist a pastor. Each senior planning on entering the ministry was assigned to a mentor pastor.

I was interviewed by Pastor Henry S. Miller from Elizabethtown, Pennsylvania. When I first met him, my impression was that we were a complete mismatch. I was very wrong. He was a very short man in a plain vest. He wore wire frame glasses and was nearly bald. I was reminded of Ichabod Crane in Washington Irving's novel, "Sleepy Hollow." But as it turned out, it was a turning point in my life. He and his wife, Sarah, became spiritual parents to Marlene and me.

Pastor Henry and Sarah Miller holding Bernice

We would travel to Elizabethtown every Sunday morning and return to Messiah College after the evening services. He would explain what was happening in the church. He asked me to preach every Sunday, taking turns on mornings and evenings. Many of my peers, involved in the same apprentice pattern, told me they only read the Scriptures or aided in worship by leading singing, but few preached as much as I was allowed. He was a most knowledgeable man. I perceived he was an avid reader. He was very wise and skilled in dealing with people.

I graduated from Messiah College in the spring of 1958. By that time Pastor Miller invited me to assist him in ministry. Marlene and I moved to Elizabethtown at the end of that summer and I became his assistant. My times with this man of God changed my life. He taught me acceptance without accommodation. It helped me understand people who disagreed with me. He modeled respect without rejection. He decreased that I might increase. He involved me beyond expectation, and he trusted me without reservation. He was an unusual mature man who believed in me as a young minister. It was a time of "chairos", a grace given to me.

Before we actually took up our responsibilities at the Elizabethtown church, we served during the summer of 1958 at Kenbrook Bible Camp. I was assistant director and camp pastor. Marlene was the camp cook. She was known as "Cookie" to Ron Long, one of the campers, who became a lifelong friend. One episode that became a memory was Marlene's vegetable soup for the campers. She had never cooked vegetable soup and so she made it with just meat and broth. So without any tomato sauce or juice it was a light green color and most of the campers fussed about it but ate it anyway. Marlene made it in spite of many negative remarks from campers for the six weeks we were there.

Howard Landis was the camp director and we had a great time. One night the two of us frightened campers and counselors in tents and it nearly cost us a reprimand when children reported to their parents. But the six weeks proved to be a rewarding experience. After six weeks of camp was over, Marlene and I were exhausted and ready to move on to Elizabethtown.

We rented a half house apartment on the north side of town. I became a student at Lancaster Theological Seminary in Lancaster, Pennsylvania. It was an interesting year. The seminary was sponsored by the Evangelical Reformed Church (now known as United Church of Christ). It had a very different theological base than my Anabaptist/Pietistic denomination, the Brethren in Christ.

I would often discuss my learning with Pastor Miller and I was amazed at his current understanding of theology and church practices. He was familiar with Carl Barth's writings and helped me understand the turns in contemporary theology. It was a great year of learning at the school, but my greatest life lessons came from Pastor Miller. He involved me in major events such as funerals and communion. He would discuss not only the Sunday worship, but what was happening in board meetings and church life. I was amazed at his grasp of church life and people. He had also served as General Secretary of the denominational Board of Administration so he shared his wisdom on general church life as well. Little did I know that later in my life much of his wisdom would come back to me when I was invited to serve the larger denomination.

I had mentioned earlier that I had not met Marlene's sister, Mary. In the fall of 1958, she returned from Africa and we had her in our home for a few days. She impressed me as a disciplined woman. I also perceived her as a very strong woman. Later I would refer to her as the family priest, since she carried a great concern for the spiritual health of all her siblings. She returned to Africa and would return to the United States six years later.

In the summer of 1959 Pastor Miller became very ill. He shared with me that he had a rheumatic heart for years. Now he was a victim of a stroke. He called Marlene and me in one day by his bedside and informed us he was going to resign. He suggested we pray about our future since he would recommend us as a potential successor. But he also noted it might be to our advantage to take another church. He said he didn't know anybody better prepared for the Elizabethtown church, but there was a history of pastors having a hard time and then leaving Elizabethtown, and he didn't want us to get hurt. It was a difficult time of decision. But we were invited in the fall of 1959 to accept the Elizabethtown pastorate. On Pastor Miller's recommendation, Bishop Henry Ginder not only installed us, but we were also ordained that September of 1959.

Chapter 12

Fatherhood

Marlene and I had decided, in light of all the developments that had occurred, we would take a year out of seminary. We also decided to begin our family. Marlene was noticeably pregnant at the time of our installation. Our first child, Bernice Elaine, was born on October 29th, 1959. It was an exciting time for us. We had moved into the parsonage just next to the church.

We had fallen in love with the church people. Three of our church members, Isaiah Bashore, Ada Engle and her daughter, Lois, lived directly across the street. They were sure they would keep tabs on us when we left for the hospital for the birth of our first child on October 29, 1959. We left in the quiet of the night. The next day I was raking leaves and Isaiah came over and asked how Marlene was doing. I informed him she and our baby girl were doing fine. Isaiah, an elderly man, completely surprised, inquired when this happened. I calmly said, "Oh, last night." He was shocked and said he was sure he would see us leave. We were watched closely by these neighbors. Marlene rejoiced that we had pulled this one off without their close observation.

After the first year, the church board encouraged me to continue my seminary training. I am not sure to this day whether they thought I really needed help or whether I felt I really needed further training. Just maybe it was both! In either case, in the fall of 1960, I entered Eastern Baptist Theological Seminary as a married student. (This seminary has been renamed Palmer Seminary.) For the next two years I would travel to Philadelphia on Tuesday mornings and return home on Friday evenings after classes. Marlene kept the home fires burning.

Every now and then she received negative feedback by the ways church people sometimes responded. Let me explain.

One event occurred with the women's organizations. There were two groups. One was called "The Daughters of the King", a group formed by the local church many years before our arrival. The other group was the "Women's Missionary Prayer Circle" formed at the suggestion of the general church's Board for World Missions. Each year they would struggle on getting officers for the two groups. I was in seminary and gaining what I thought was insight. I came up with the idea of combining the two groups. It would only take one slate of officers and save all the hassle they usually had trying to find two groups of officers. I suggested to my wife that she could propose my suggestion at their next meeting.

Well, when Marlene made the suggestion of combining the two groups, one of the women (an acknowledged leader of the church women) asked for a time of prayer on their knees. She prayed that the two groups would never join. When I returned home from seminary, my wife made it clear that any suggestion I had for change in the future would come from me, not her! I was learning about marriage as well as church leading dynamics.

Those were two busy years going to seminary and being the pastor of our church. I had local retired ministers or neighboring pastors care for the midweek services and I would preach twice on Sundays and also chair the church board meetings and any other groups before heading off to seminary very early each Tuesday morning.

As you might guess, there were times when I was weary and would get sleepy. One early morning I saw red lights, which I thought was a slow truck. It turned out to be an Amish buggy. I braked hard and nearly collided. When I arrived at seminary some classmates said I looked pale. All I can say is that I am grateful to God for sparing me in a couple of close calls.

During my senior year of seminary we decided to try for a second child. When I informed the church board of this decision, one of the older men took me aside and told me children weren't planned, they just came. He obviously didn't know about birth control, nor understood my wife, but I thanked him for his wisdom. Bruce Eric was born on December 6th, 1961. Marlene has always said she knew I wanted a son and when they wheeled her out on the gurney, she looked at me and said, "That's it!" I suggested we could discuss it later, but she had made a final decision.

We were now blest with two healthy children, Bernice and Bruce. They provided us much joy and also seemed to make many of the older members of our church more solicitous of us. They were the first grandchildren on my side of the family. So my parents were doting grandparents when they had the opportunity. Marlene's widowed mother was in Kansas.

One point of tension in our marriage was seeing my parents and family much more than Marlene could visit her mother. So one summer she had the opportunity to travel west with some people. She took the two children and planned to spend a week with her mother. As it turned out, I was having some dental issues and I had to delay my trip to pick them up two weeks later. I had what they call "dry socket" from a tooth being pulled. It is really painful and slow healing.

By the time I could travel and pick them up, she informed me she was really glad to see me which made me feel good since I was so lonely for her and our children. She related to me that her mother and she had words about child rearing. She never raised the issue of visiting her mother again. I also kept my mouth shut about our visits to my parents.

After I completed seminary, I began suggesting changes for the church. One move I made was to suggest that the church building needed some improvements. I also thought it would be easier to attract new people if we made some changes to our facilities. I suggested a building fund and the church board approved it. At the end of the first year, we only had $50.00 in the fund. Marlene and I had made that donation. I was disappointed, but not discouraged.

Not many months after that, we had a new couple come to our congregation and they stayed. They suggested to me that we needed to make some changes to the facility to attract new people. I asked them to speak to the church board members. At a later board meeting one of the members proposed making some changes to the building. I quickly affirmed the idea and to my amazement the project grew quickly and thousands of dollars were received that year to begin the remodeling. I was learning that it works far better if the local church leaders own the idea and they propose changes.

It was a good time in our marriage and family. We basked in the loving role of being young parents. We have many memories of our children growing from infants to young children.

They provided us with a few exciting dramas. On one occasion they were playing in the basement and somehow Bruce spilled some Clorox on his head and even ingested some. He had it in his eyes and also needed his stomach pumped, which necessitated an emergency trip to the hospital. The doctor was concerned about scars in his eyes. Fortunately, he was not seriously harmed. Due to the pumping of his stomach, it took a long time before he would open his mouth in a doctor's office.

Another time the two were left for a few moments in the car and somehow released the brake and it coasted into an empty burning barrel with no one hurt. But mostly it was pleasant times with both Bernice and Bruce providing us with the joy of family life.

I was having an exciting time developing sermon series and helping the church to grow. It was a good time in our lives. Our children were loved and nourished by the congregation. I was feeling fulfilled and challenged in being a pastor.

Another life enhancing process during these years at Elizabethtown was meeting with a group of peers, pastor friends, and spouses. It included John and Eva Brubaker, Clark and Miriam Hock, Roy and Lois Jean Peterman and Marlene and me. As I recall, we would meet about once a month. The women would often gather in one room and discuss important issues. We pastors often talked church and of course shared our wisdom about our bishop. I have a memory of Clark Hock, at one of our meetings, suggesting we each read a book and discuss it. That led to one memorable time when we each wrote a short paper describing the role of a pastor. The result of that meeting was fascinating. It really ended up with each of us describing our strengths and gifts as we saw ourselves. John Brubaker described himself as a minister. Roy Peterman focused on being an evangelist. Clark Hock wrote about himself as being in the prophetic role. I wrote about my role as a pastor/teacher. It was an eye opener that enabled us to appreciate each of our differences, and we affirmed each role as being significant and helpful to our respective churches.

An interesting dynamic was being a pastor to some of my peers from my college days. We became good friends of the J. Harold Engle family. His father, Martin Engle, was a lay leader and a member of the church board. I often felt odd when his father would refer to him as a child, knowing I was the same age. But it was well meant and Martin always had respect for my role as pastor. It was really hard when I had to deal with confrontation of some of my peers who sought me for counsel on delicate issues. One young man who had been a classmate in college was seeking to be a minister. He came to me and confessed he and his girlfriend were expecting a baby before their marriage.

It was a challenge to deal with such relationships. I was getting help in seminary, but real life in the parish was beyond some of my training. My wife, home church pastor, college teachers, my mentor Henry Miller, and my bishop were all helpful in dealing with many of the pastoral challenges I faced.

I also was involved with the local ministerial group where I met pastors of other denominations and observed differing opinions on issues in the community. The Lutheran pastor was a believer in *comity*, which was a concept that our small town had enough churches and he was not pleased about the Southern Baptists coming to town.

I was more respectful of the Church of the Brethren pastor who was more open. It was his opinion that we should welcome any new churches, discerning that we had so many community people who were not involved in any church so any new churches that could serve them would be welcomed.

We would share in community services at Thanksgiving time. It was a way of helping our people become more aware of other churches. Over the years the Brethren in Christ had kept to themselves, but now we were seeing other churches as our allies and not competition or a threat. I had been encouraged by my mentor Henry Miller to involve our church in the community. One year I preached at the Lutheran church and the pastor outfitted me in a robe and white surplice with a cross hanging from my neck. Some of our people thought it looked great but a few hinted that I might be losing my faith. I also served as an officer for a while in the local ministerial association.

Before I move on with my journey, I will share a few stories about pastoral acts that every minister has experienced, but with a few unique accents.

I always believed it was an honor to lead Holy Communion. During my years in the pastorate we only held those four times a year. Some of our churches have gone to more frequent communion observances which I believe is a good thing. One memorable year during Holy Week at Elizabethtown, I planned a different approach. I had found an artist's conception of a drawing of each of the twelve disciples and a drawing of the Christ. These were placed at a long table in the midst of grapes and communion bread and individual cups of grape juice. I had the people come twelve at a time and sit by each of the drawings except the Christ where we left an empty chair. I wondered how a number of the older members would handle this change. At the close, one elderly lady sidled up to me and said, "Pastor there was only one thing wrong with this communion." I prepared myself for a blast of criticism. Instead she quietly said, "You didn't allow enough time at the table." I was learning. On Worldwide Communion Sunday we often invited international students from Messiah College to share with us and I would invite them to have prayers at the table.

I only had a few funerals at Elizabethtown. One was for an elderly lady whom I visited often even as I attended seminary. One day she asked me how old I was and when I informed her I was only twenty-something she exclaimed, "Why you are just a kid!" She was right. She honored me to conduct and preach at her memorial service.

One of her sons attended another church and his pastor was to have a prayer. Well, he spoke longer than me and used loud and accusatory language for some of the family he intimated had strayed from mother's ways.

I rode with the Funeral Director to the graveside. He asked me where this other minister came from. I told him he was new to me and it was a conservative church. He said, "Well you, like most ministers, sounded like a symphony of comfort, but this man banged the cymbals!" I told him he was to have a prayer at the grave. He said, "Well we might have a resurrection." As it turned out, the visiting minister gave a very short quiet prayer and my prayers were answered.

One other funeral was for a total stranger. The Funeral Director called and asked if I would conduct a service at the funeral home. I agreed. The Director alerted me the widow had a reputation and it was well known of her involvement with other men. But I should be prepared for an outburst of tears and loud grief. He implied it would not be genuine. He was right, but I quietly led the service and pointed the group to Jesus. She did give a few outbursts but it went well. I was still learning.

I enjoyed weddings more than any other pastoral act. There were a couple of weddings at the church that are memorable. One of the first marriages was our organist, Joyce Hilsher, to Ron Miller. After the ceremony a fellow minister told me he did not like my changing the wording of the ceremony from the old English to a more colloquial version. I received his comments but was glad I accommodated the bride's and groom's choice of wording.

Another marriage was college student friends Marlin Hess and Trudy Good. They were living in Cumberland County, Pennsylvania, but they came to Lancaster County for the ceremony. After the wedding, I learned in seminary that, in Pennsylvania, the marriage license needs to be secured in the county in which the marriage is officiated. I asked the professor after class if I had married them illegally. He informed me that unless there was a major divorce over great sums of money, it was likely not worth redoing the paper work. So the issue was dropped.

I officiated at the wedding of three of my siblings, Thelma and Barry, Sam and Mary, and Doris and Danny. I was very young and was honored to be a part of the beginnings of their married lives.

In the case of my sister, Thelma, after years of working at their marriage, Barry decided to leave and remarry. My sister handled this really well. It was a difficult time for her and her three children. After her three children were adults and years later, she remarried Bill Hummer. I will update some special times with Thelma and Bill in my senior years.

Also, after I left the pastorate I performed marriages with two of Marlene's nieces. The one was Mary (Engle) Rock. It was held in Kansas and I was bishop at the time. The pastor said just before the wedding, I'm sure you have a Kansas license to perform marriage. I said, "What are you talking about?" He informed me the state of Kansas required ministers to register at the courthouse. It was Saturday afternoon. We called and the courthouse was open until later. So after I had pronounced Mary and Kent husband and wife, I hurried into town with my wife and signed the book. The women in the Abilene, Kansas Court House knew of the wedding and asked if it was already over. I responded, "Yes, and is there a time on the license?" They said no and we all agreed not to tell.

I had a bit of fun with my frugal wife. When I returned to the car where she waited, I said this license is good for the rest of my life. It only cost $100! Before she could explain how we could not afford this, I quickly informed her it was only a $1.00 fee.

We both agreed that was one of the least expensive fees we ever paid for a license.

The other niece, Jessica (Engle) Snyder, invited me to have her wedding and her father, Millard, my wife's youngest brother, arranged for her beloved puppy dog to be the ring bearer. It was a first for me. It was a total surprise and it went very well.

It was an honor to be invited to conduct the marriage ceremony for my youngest sister's daughter, Jenny Arbaugh, and her husband Paul. It was unique since it was held on a long staircase in a theatre in Fort Wayne, Indiana. They wanted to share glasses of wine as a symbol of their unity. I had a little fun telling the attendants I feared they expected me to turn water into wine as Jesus had done at a wedding he attended. It was a really good celebration. My wife and I danced, a first for us, since that was forbidden in our church culture.

Since I spent most of my years in church administration, these times of celebration of life and death were few. But they have left me with many memories.

We did stay at Elizabethtown until the summer of 1965.

Chapter 13

Family

The celebrations of the holidays were special since I always planned to be home during those occasions. Christmas has always been a special time for us. Our children often remember such things as the "Jesse Tree" with prophetic words about the coming of Christ. We hung symbols on a bare-branched tree. And we had a model train garden in our different homes that may have been my hobby, but the family enjoyed it.

We also had some summer camping trips with the Brubakers and other friends in the area along Lake Michigan. We camped with Charlie Byers Jr. and his family in southern Indiana. Our family was blest with the memories of those pleasant vacations.

My youngest sister, Nancy (14 years younger), came after her senior year in high school to spend a summer with us in Nappanee, Indiana. She and my wife would want different music on the radio, so Marlene told her whoever got to the radio first in the morning could set the station. My sister Nancy learned it is hard to get ahead of Marlene!

One memorable time at the sand dunes along Lake Michigan was an evening of camping. During the setting up of the tent, my wedding band flew off my finger and into the sand. I felt it go and saw the general area and we drew a big circle. We found a small sifter in the nearby camp store and proceeded to sift sand to find the ring. As it got later into the evening and we were still sifting sand, my sister said, "If people in white coats show up, I will say I don't know you." We were about to give up and then, there it was in the sifter. I still have the ring today!

It was a good summer for my sister and she helped Marlene with our children when I was gone. Marlene did fix a meal my sister never experienced. It consisted of hard-boiled eggs, fried potatoes, and cold stewed tomatoes. My sister called it a "depression meal."

Our family enjoyed camping. During our earlier years in Pennsylvania we started camping in a 10 foot by 12 foot canvas tent. One time while I was away from our home in California, Marlene bought a small trailer camper with a canvas top. This got us off the ground but the only amenity was an icebox, so we still used our other camping equipment from the tent days. It was using this small trailer that we visited many campgrounds in California, Oregon, Washington, Arizona, Utah, New Mexico and Nevada. Our kids enjoyed these adventures. We also took in numerous National Parks. Then, just as our kids started leaving home, we purchased our first small motor home, a Toyota Odyssey that was well equipped. Marlene and I enjoyed using this as a get away from my busy schedule with pastors and churches.

Later we went from the small motor home to our first fifth wheel; a 19-foot Alpenlite and pulled it with a very light pickup truck, a General Motors Company S15. The truck was almost too light. Our second fifth wheel was an Alfa Sun, a 27-footer, and we then moved to a half-ton pickup truck. Our third fifth wheel, a 33-foot Sea Breeze, was really a luxury with three slide-outs. Our kids have reminded us frequently how I would point out these big rigs when we were in our tent camping days and tell them that in a rig that big you may as well stay home. Camping was our favorite family past time.

Another adventure was the acquisition of a dog. This is the only dog we have had in over fifty-six years of married life. Our daughter had been frightened when she was about two years old by a barking dog that knocked her down when we lived in Elizabethtown, Pennsylvania. Our friends at Nappanee encouraged us to get a dog to help Bernice's fear.

One day our pastor's wife, Barbara Bert, saw a note in the local laundromat of a poodle for sale. We checked it out and it was a larger dog than I had pictured in my mind. The family that had it was divided. The wife wanted to get rid of the dog, but her husband and son wanted to keep it. In light of the conflict in the home, we told them we would think it over.

On the way home, our two children were excited and disappointed in my not taking the dog. Bruce and Bernice made it abundantly clear they wanted the dog. When the lady called the next day and offered the dog and all his belongings for $15, we made the trip to pick him up. The man hid behind a newspaper and wouldn't talk with us; the son had locked himself and the dog in his bedroom. Well, his mother eventually got the dog and we took him home.

We called him "Pepe." We had a veterinarian, Ed Meyers, in our local church and we took Pepe to him for a checkup. The previous owners led us to believe he was a young dog, but the vet said they must have turned the mileage back on his speedometer. He checked him out and we had him neutered. He was a good dog and I came to like him as much as any of the family. I hoped to keep the dog but as it turned out we did not take "Pepe" to California.

Just before our move to California, Marlene and I discussed moving the dog. She left me know she did not want a dog in our next house. I finally said if she could persuade our children to leave Pepe in Indiana, I would agree to it. I thought I had won this difference between us since the kids were really fond of the dog. I came home from a trip and, at the evening meal, I asked if we were taking Pepe to California. Both children dropped their heads. I asked again and after a long silence Marlene said the children were agreed to leave Pepe behind. I questioned them and sadly they said their Mother was right.

It was not until years later Marlene finally confessed she had told our children Pepe wouldn't be able to make the trip and it would be better to leave him behind. I still don't understand how she convinced them, but they had a strong love and trust in their mother. I, of course, questioned her wisdom on what she told them, but she said, "Well what if Pepe would die on the trip?" I just looked at her shaking my head and still can't understand the logic of my wife.

Well, we tried to sell the dog. When that didn't work, we tried giving him away. Finally after all options ran out, one night we took him to the animal shelter in Elkhart, Indiana. It was a sad time, and we told the children to stay in the car. But Bruce was curious and came in the door just as they were leading his beloved Pepe away with a rope on his neck. I told them we would go see a Disney movie. As it turned out it was "Old Yeller." If you have seen that film you know it is a very sad dog story. The family was in tears. When asked by the children, "Why this movie?" I said, "Let us all leave." We did. That was a time of good old dad losing all the way.

Another hobby that developed during the years at Upland was my interest in purchasing a motorcycle. My wife was adamantly against this venture. I took our son Bruce to look at some Honda bikes. We were both convinced it would be a fine addition to our family. My wife still said, no! Then I informed Bruce we needed to take her along shopping. Now, that is a man's logic and it worked. She looked them over and we convinced her we would just buy a small bike, and she agreed to us buying a Honda 200.

I really impressed her when I went to purchase insurance, lost my balance in the parking lot, fell over and banged my head on the asphalt after removing my helmet.

I entered the business office of our insurance agent and he asked if I knew my head was bleeding. When I reached up and discovered an abrasion, I decided to be honest and explained my fall in the parking lot. He asked, with an incredible look on his face, "You want me to insure you as a rider of this bike?"

Marlene tried operating the bike when I was away and she ran into a tree and the garage and damaged it more than I had in the parking lot. She would not operate it again and I had hopes of us each having our own bikes in the future.

Sometime later, she did agree to me getting a larger bike, a Honda 550. I had not foreseen the possibility that when our son became a driver, he would want to ride the motorcycle. So now my male logic was that a larger bike would be safer for Bruce on the freeways! She looked doubtful, but reluctantly agreed; I think because she saw how desperately I wanted the larger bike. It was an incredibly powerful and sleek machine. Our son Bruce, years later would say, "It was a nice bike!" Marlene would ride with me.

Then, our friends, Calvin and Pat Pannebecker, urged us to buy a larger street bike and we purchased a used 1100 Honda Gold Wing. We would go riding with our friends. The longest trip was a ride with Calvin as far as Las Vegas, Nevada. He went on really long rides like from Canada to Mexico and he wanted me to join him, but I declined. It was a bit much for me and my wife wasn't excited about me going.

When we later moved back east we sold that bike, but it gave us many pleasant adventures in California. I only laid it down once in gravel up at the base of Mt. Baldy but with no serious injury.

Having a motorcycle challenged some people's image of a bishop. I offered my colleague, Bishop Henry Ginder, a ride, but he declined since it reminded him of Hell's Angels! I think he was more concerned about his image.

My predecessor, Arthur Climenhaga, however accepted my invitation for a ride and risked his reputation. Most folk seemed to appreciate my free spirit.

Several family accidents happened when I was away on church work. Bruce asked me before I left on a trip I made to Oklahoma, if he could build a ramp out of some wood in the garage. He wanted to jump it with his bicycle. I gave him my permission. Marlene called me on the weekend and said, everything is all right now, but Bruce has a broken arm and collar bone. Apparently he was showing his sister and her friends how he could jump his bicycle off the ramp "taking air" as he put it, but the ramp broke and he tumbled in the air landing on concrete and thus the broken boy.

Another traumatic incident happened near Christmas one year when our daughter, who had recently acquired a driver's license, with a car full of teenage friends had an accident at an intersection and totaled the car. No one was hurt and my wife informed me after I arrived home. I should mention my wife also had an accident at an intersection and fortunately no one was injured.

In the case of Bernice, we were summoned to court and I heard the judge yelling at a young man who exited his chambers, and I was really apprehensive about what he would say to our daughter. I warned her to steel herself for the confrontation and I would support her even though the police report indicated she was at fault. When we were asked in, he looked us over. He asked Bernice a few questions. She told him she was distracted by friends and Christmas lights at the intersection. I expected him to explode with severe reprimands.

Instead, he looked at me and informed me that women were better drivers than men. I'm not sure why this fact was brought up but I was in no position to question it. He informed me more with a mini lecture as if I needed help understanding.

He then told our daughter if passengers in a car were distracting, pull over and ask them to leave. Then he levied a fine of $15.00 and dismissed us.

On the way out, our daughter exclaimed, "Gee, Dad, that wasn't so bad." I almost said something negative, but instead we went home. She reported to her mother who enjoyed hearing how women were better drivers. I inquired how that could be when they both totaled cars. In Marlene's case she thought she was at a four-way stop intersection, but it was a two-way stop. When she proceeded, the oncoming car accidentally hit her. The man who hit her was an illegal immigrant with no license and no insurance. The police never mentioned she was at fault and the insurance took care of it. In logic, that only women can understand, she informed me the judge knew more about women drivers than I did! I was and am still learning the ways of women.

Two Children and Spouses, 1986,
Bob and Bernice and Bruce and Carol

In 1982 Marlene's family began gathering at regular Engle Family reunions. These became a delightful time of learning to know her extended family. The family had gathered in 1977 for a wedding and then it was decided to meet in Estes Park, Colorado in 1982. We have gathered about every three years over the last three decades. The setting in the Rocky Mountains is gorgeous and the time with family has always been a rich experience.

The Shafer clan gathered less frequently for reunions. We have had several memorable occasions which have involved my brother's boat or yacht club as a setting. We have also gathered at his home.

Chapter 14

Church Administration

It was in the early part of 1965 that I was asked to serve on a committee to select a new Director of Sunday Schools for our denomination. The two men with whom I was asked to serve were our local physician, Dr. Harold H. Engle, and a college professor, Dr. Arthur Climenhaga. I was surprised to be serving with such two older, experienced and lettered men. I was even more shocked to discover, P. W. McBeth, who was a member of the Elizabethtown church, would be leaving his post. They wanted to know if I had any ideas of younger men who would be qualified to take his place. I recall suggesting several of my peers.

And then they said they had a suggestion. I quickly, maybe too quickly, said their ideas would be fine with me. At that point they suggested my name. I couldn't believe my ears. I had not pictured myself in such a role. It was my thought that I would be a pastor all my life, and I planned to stay at Elizabethtown as long as I could.

Well, as it evolved, I was invited to accept the role. After counsel with a number of people, my wife and I agreed to accept. It meant a move and a real change in direction. Our local church board did not want to accept my resignation. Bishop Ginder met with the Church Board and informed them it was our decision to leave. One man came to me and wondered if more salary would change our minds. We were affirmed by such a response, but we decided to take the new call of the church.

In my new role as Director of Sunday Schools, the Board of Christian Education wanted me to be located at a church office. The Brethren in Christ denomination was seeking a place to name as church headquarters, so we were moved to Palmyra, Pennsylvania on a temporary basis. The Palmyra Brethren in Christ church had a vacant house next to the church where I had my office for a year. We rented a house from a school teacher on the east side of Harrisburg, Pennsylvania, who was away for six weeks of study. He and his family returned and we actually lived in a tent for a week. Then Marlene and our children stayed in my father's cabin in the Allegheny Mountains near Mercersburg, Pennsylvania for two weeks while I was on the road in church work. Then we rented another teacher's house in Palmyra who was away for the best part of the year.

During my time on the road working for the Board of Christian Education, I often stayed in private homes. One of my first stays was in the home of Clarence Boyer who was concerned that I would be worthy of my new assignment. He was a staunch admirer of P. W. McBeth, my predecessor. He affirmed me as I left their home and assured me I would do a great work for our church. This comment of approval coming from this well respected churchman was most encouraging.

During the year at Palmyra, Dr. C. N. Hostetter, former president of Messiah College, was the pastor. My wife related well with his wife who had been a shy lady and not seen much at the college. Our children also enjoyed the church activities of Palmyra.

In the first year in Christian Education I worked closely with Walter Winger from Canada. Our combination of gifts enabled us to travel to various congregations and together we presented a call to our churches to get a more unified curriculum for Sunday Schools and a solid youth program.

Eber Dourte, Don Shafer, and Walter Winger

Eber Dourte also worked with us on Home and Family Education. Walter was also part-time pastor of a small church in Canada. Walter and I would meet from time to time at a motel in Bath, New York, and spend a day and night dreaming and planning our work together. It was an exciting time.

Once in western Pennsylvania we stayed in a private home. The house was not very clean. Walter usually liked to sleep in and I would like to get up and get going. Thus I was surprised when the lady of the house asked when we wanted breakfast and Walter said as soon as it suits you in the morning.

Then we found out we had to pour water from a bucket to flush the commode. And Walter suspected we might encounter bed bugs. I was laughing and he informed me this was serious business, so I tried to sober up. In the morning the woman had homemade bread and I thought it tasted a bit odd, but I praised her for the homemade bread. The eggs she served were not quite done, but I experienced that before. After our farewells and we were in our vehicle, I turned to Walter and asked why he kicked me under the table. He asked me if I had never had rancid butter before. I said, "No, what is it?" He informed me not to talk about this until after lunch, visibly upset. I wanted to laugh, but decided the better part of wisdom was to be half serious. He later informed me rancid butter was soured and spoiling. And then he asked why I kept praising her? I had no good response. He informed me I was something less than intelligent.

On one of our trips across the United States we stayed in a home in northern Kansas where the wife was a Canadian and the husband a Unites States citizen. They had a photo of President John Kennedy and a second photo of Queen Elizabeth hanging in their home. I asked their young son who the two people were. He was just learning to talk and he quickly responded, "Oh, him is president "Tennedy" (Kennedy) and she is him sister!" I nearly split a gut, but Walter was not amused. In fact he knew me well enough to advise me not to tell that story in Canada. Well, that only encouraged me and I told it at Niagara Christian College later on that trip. The students there enjoyed it more than Walter appreciated

On that same trip we had a bit of conflict over our differences in driving. One night I got sleepy. I tried to get Walter awake but it was futile. I kept driving, dozed off and ran off the road into the center grassy section of the highway. It brought Walter up and I recall him saying something about no trees, and get this thing back on the highway. It was a bit scary but it did get us both wide awake and I got the vehicle under control. It led to a tense conversation in which Walter made some critical remarks about my driving. We argued about our driving tendencies, but in the end we agreed not to tell our superiors upon our return.

Dr. Harold Engle (our Executive Director at the time) approached me and asked about our trip. I gave him a short reply that the churches received us well and we had a safe trip. I was surprised when he then said he heard a different story from Walter. I felt betrayed and Dr. Engle asked for my version, so I shared. When I confronted Walter, he passed it off as unimportant. It was about this time the Board of Christian Education decided to employ an Executive Director. I suggested to Dr. Engle that, since Walter was a bit older and more experienced, perhaps they should call him; but Dr. Engle said the board wanted me and he would inform Walter.

I soon heard Walter had interviewed to become a pastor at Carlisle, Pennsylvania. Walter was a bit cool, but he affirmed me then and later when I became bishop. He also was affirming when I became General Secretary. We had many differences, but I always considered him a friend. We met as couples several times. Our families also shared some time on the shores and waters of Lake Erie and later on Walter took me in his boat on the Niagara River. Walter was an adventurous soul.

Many years later Walter was invited to pastor the Upland Brethren in Christ church in California. He asked if we could talk and I met him and his wife, Lois, and encouraged them to accept the Upland pastorate. It was during his years at Upland, he felt I left him down when I would not take sides when he was involved in conflict at Upland. We had lunch about once a month and often disagreed on issues, but I would affirm our friendship. I regret he developed feelings that were not positive about our relationship. As for me, I can only wish he had discussed the issues and we could likely have resolved differences from my perspective, but he chose otherwise. In my journey of life I have always wanted to resolve conflicts but I was learning it always takes two and sometimes you just have to let things rest.

In the late summer of 1966, we moved to Nappanee, Indiana. The denomination had settled on the Evangel Publishing House located there as the address of our general church headquarters. My office would be located there. Our move to Nappanee, Indiana was tough for my parents because we had been living within an hour or so driving distance from them, and now we would be over 500 miles away. It was a turn in our journey that would affect our life and outlook.

Nappanee is a small Midwest town just east of South Bend, Indiana. So we became fans of the Notre Dame Football team for the seasons over the next six years. Nappanee was an accepting community. We loved the spring and fall; they had really beautiful "Indian Summers." However, the winters were long and mostly overcast since we were in proximity to the weather off of Lake Michigan. Our children remember the winters as being bitterly cold.

Our first house was a rental property, a former manse owned by the United Methodist church. The trustees of this rental were not always prompt. One winter when I was away, the snow and ice built up on the flat roof over our laundry and kitchen. It leaked down over our recently purchased washer and my wife gave the trustees a sermon they would not soon forget, likely more memorable than their pastor's sermons! We were there until we purchased the first house in our married life.

It was a two-story older house on Van Buren Street and we enjoyed fixing up the garage, bathroom, and kitchen to suit our needs. It was a pleasant neighborhood. We did have a small shed in the backyard and once some pranksters painted a half moon on it and dumped it over. I secured it in concrete and it stayed there. But mostly, we have warm memories of our neighbors.

Even better, we were now located a couple of blocks closer to John and Eva Brubaker's family who also lived on the west side of Nappanee. John was my associate in my work as Executive Director of Christian Education. We related in mutual ways and complemented each other in our work. We became family friends—a relationship that has continued since those days. As a matter of fact, since our move back to California in 2000, we now live within an hour's driving time to the Brubakers' home.

We were also close friends with the Erwin and Lois Thomas family. We would often ride bicycles with them and then stop at the local "B and B" restaurant for pie and coffee. We also related to John and Nellie Hostetter and John and Alice Grace Zercher and their family. Since my office was at Evangel Press we learned to know many of the employees.

Marlene first worked in the local bank. Then a few years later she went to work for the Water Company of Nappanee. She enjoyed her work and the community. During these years I was gone about fifty percent of the time, so Marlene really had a major role in raising our two children and taking care of the facility of our house. She provided a loving atmosphere for our home. She did a great job of handling our finances at home and was a great mother and housekeeper. Her excellent work as a parent would show up later as our children matured, married and had their own families. Marlene was really showing the strength my Dad had perceived. She has been and is a great lover, mother, financier, and manager.

During our years in Nappanee, our daughter, Bernice, was three years ahead of Bruce in school. Marlene with two young children was also working. The Brubakers had three children, and we were good friends doing numerous things together. With John and me on the road, the two women were supportive of each other.

Marlene recalls one cold winter when I was away on church work. She and our son Bruce were delivering newspapers and it was so cold they both nearly had frostbite on their toes and fingers. She called Eva who helped them with a car to finish the route.

During these six years I learned much about the general church. As Executive Director of the Board of Christian Education, later named Board of Congregational Life, I learned to know many of the church leaders, both board members and clergy. Working with the regional bishops was also very interesting.

At one point we had devised a plan called, "Congregational Analysis Program." We had put together a booklet that local churches would fill out, and then a colleague and I would work with the bishop of the area where the church was located. We conducted over twenty-five of these congregational evaluation projects between 1971 and 1972. The purpose of these projects was to help the local church discover their purpose and then lay plans for growth and development.

During one of these projects I questioned Bishop Henry Ginder about a response on evangelism. The consultation at that point included the bishop, John Brubaker, me and the local pastor. I was asking for a more specific response than a general answer, but Bishop Ginder apparently thought I was challenging his expertise. He was obviously not pleased, excused himself and suggested I could finish the session. Well, my colleague, John Brubaker, looked at me, the pastor seemed amused, and John wondered aloud what we would do now? I excused myself, found Bishop Ginder, and apologized, explaining I didn't mean to challenge him and strongly urged him to return to the group. He did and we were able to resume our project.

I was relieved and also learning about church politics the hard way. Later, Dr. Robert Smith, then Chairman of the Board of Christian Education, explained to me the psychology of "territorialism" and observed I had entered a bullpen where I was not expected and the bull bounced me out. It was an insight I remembered and his counsel served me well then and later. Dr. Smith was a psychiatrist and I valued his insights.

There were also times of unexpected moments in private homes. On a trip to Virginia, John Brubaker and I were being hosted in a family travel trailer. It was not hooked up with water, so we were to use the church facilities and, since there was no hot water, if we wanted a shower to go to the house. In the morning I decided on a shower. As I entered the house the father and several children were waiting for the school bus. He informed me the bathroom was not occupied so I went in and proceeded to shower and shave.

I did note that there were three doors in the bathroom that also served as a laundry room. It seemed a bit unusual, but I was only interested in the door from which I came in. I was shaving at the sink stripped to my waist. Suddenly the pastor's wife, still in a very modest nightgown and in a sleepy daze opened the door beside the sink. It happened so suddenly I didn't respond until she patted me on my tummy, and headed for the commode behind me. I immediately spoke loudly, saying, "Excuse me!" She screamed and made a hasty retreat.

I stood there looking in the mirror and then chuckled to myself. Then I mused about what I would say as I returned outside to the trailer. Or what in the world I would say to her husband on my way out the front door? Her husband was sitting in the living room. He didn't look up from reading the newspaper and I informed him I was finished in the bathroom, knowing he had to have heard his wife scream, and I wondered what he was thinking. He just quietly said, "Thank you."

Anyway, I went to the camper trailer and related the incident to John. He looked at me and asked, "Do you think she thought you were her husband?" "Well John," I replied, "I surely hope so!" We both laughed. Then he asked, "How will we handle this on the way to breakfast?" I told him I didn't know and wondered if he had any suggestions.

We were meeting a group of pastors and wives with the regional bishop. In the car we talked about the weather and plans for the day. But I was sure we were all thinking about the bathroom episode.

As it turned out, we were early and after making arrangements with the restaurant manager we were alone in the meeting room. So I boldly, said, "Uh, about what happened in the bathroom, it was just an unplanned happening and I wouldn't tell the story with anyone's names, except among those of us present." The husband quickly explained that he had planned to get locks on the doors. John turned to the window and remarked how beautiful the view was. The wife was blushing bright red and the subject was dropped. The bishop arrived and that was the end until years later. When I returned home, my wife nearly split laughing and hoped she would not do such a thing. I told her it wasn't too hard to take.

Nappanee was a quiet small town and we enjoyed the culture and pace of life. The so called "Indian Summers" in late fall were often very pleasant. Many neighbors would burn leaves along the street and I loved the pungent smell, knowing it was a sign that winter would soon be on its way. One year we had to replace a sewer line from the house to the street since roots of the numerous maple trees on our corner had invaded the sewer line. It was an expensive project but we never had the problem again.

During these years I traveled a lot. Bishop John Hostetter and his wife Nellie frequently had us to their home. On one occasion, Nellie and Marlene were talking about packing for their husbands. Nellie informed Marlene that one time after John remarked about his suitcase not being packed right, she determined she would clean his clothes, fold them and then told John to pack his own suitcase. My wife thought this was a great idea and so from then on I packed my own bags. My wife liked Nellie and her forthright responses to her husband John. I was still learning about men and women! The trouble was my wife was also learning about dealing with marriage when a husband travelled and she learned fast.

Then in the late winter or early spring of 1972 on a trip to Pennsylvania I was asked whether I would allow my name to be placed in nomination for bishop of the Midwest and Pacific Conferences. It was an affirming and exciting possibility for me. For my wife it meant leaving a comfortable job, good community, loving congregation and our friends. She knew I wanted to take this and was supportive, but she left me know some things that we might have to face. Marlene always has a way of keeping my feet on solid ground and being very realistic. My spirituality has never impressed her!

We did consult numerous friends and church leaders. One phone call from my previous Bishop, Henry Ginder, was interesting. He left me know he was aware of my nomination and then encouraged me to accept since he thought they needed a younger man on the team. The way he put it was some of the older men had been barking up the same tree for so long that sometimes they weren't sure what they were barking at. That amazed me as well as his confidence in inviting me on the team. When I became a colleague he treated me as an equal with mutual respect. Apparently this time I was invited into his territory and he actually wanted me there.

I found him to be a supportive leader in what was to become my new role. The invitation was a challenge, somewhat scary, but also very alluring. In the end we accepted and in July of 1972, Marlene and I were consecrated as a young bishop and wife. This called for a move to Upland, California.

At the General Conference in early July, 1972, just prior to our move, the Board of Christian Education planned a farewell for me. I was really feeling sad since Marlene felt she couldn't take off work and afford the days away and decided she could not be at this celebration. She had been so supportive and I wanted her to hear any comments and inform the group of her contribution to my life. I was so surprised when she walked in just as the event was underway. I stood and uttered, "Holy Cow," not really a good remark for a man about to be consecrated as a bishop. But the group there enjoyed my unedited comment. Marlene came and gave me a warm hug and a kiss and joined me for the celebration. The board had arranged for Lester Haines, a churchman and private pilot, to fly her down and back so she missed very little work. I enjoyed my work in Christian Education. It gave me an overview of the church in both Canada and the United States.

I should note I enjoyed working with my colleague John Brubaker. He had been employed as my assistant after Walter Winger left. John and I were compatible in many ways. He was better at details and I worked more with planning and creative ways of communication. Or another way to explain it would be to say John was more task oriented and I was more relational oriented so together we drew on each other's strengths.

One of our interesting contrasts was in personality. He was a "night person" and I was an "early morning" person. It made for some interesting travel times. One very early morning we were leaving Nappanee, Indiana for Harrisburg, Pennsylvania and had been driving for miles. I was talking rapidly when John interrupted me and said, "Excuse me, Don, I haven't heard a word you have said and I need some coffee before I can function well." So I thanked him for helping me understand and we stopped for breakfast and then, after sufficient coffee, John was ready for mutual conversation. One of the hardest parts of deciding to accept the office of bishop was losing this friendly, working relationship, but we have kept in touch over the years. To this day we enjoy being together and our spouses add to the friendship.

Chapter 15

Bishop

After being consecrated as a bishop along with my spouse, Marlene, our family of four moved from Nappanee, Indiana to Upland, California in the summer of 1972. Our daughter who was then turning to a teenager (thirteen) was reluctant to leave her friends in Nappanee. On the other hand we had previously taken them on vacation to California in 1970 and our son, Bruce, who was turning eleven, remembered Disneyland, so he was ready to move. But when the actual move came, I remember Bruce riding with me in the rental truck our first day on the road and seeing tears roll down his cheek; I inquired what was wrong. He said, "Dad I just left all my friends behind in Nappanee!" I tried to console him.

As we stopped at different places I often called *tourist traps,* Bruce spotted mounted cattle horns and wanted to buy them. So, over his mother's protest, we finally purchased them. The purchase helped him look to the future. To this day we aren't sure what happened to those horns. I suspect my wife managed to pass those on discreetly to some thrift store but she seldom remembers how such things disappeared.

Bernice, after arriving in California, and quickly making new friends at school soon loved the west. Bernice and Bruce adjusted to the California lifestyle and both eventually became residents of California after they met the loves of their lives and got married. And they would both, with their spouses, have two children each and become California families.

Marlene and I had made a trip to California prior to our move and, with the help of her brother, LG, purchased a house located at 865 Sharon Way in Upland, a couple blocks north of the Upland church and very close to the Upland senior high school. We lived in that house for twenty years, the longest stay in any one house in our married life. It was about 1,600 square feet, but it was adequate for us. Both of our children had their own bedroom and we had a spacious living room with a small family room as well.

House in Upland, CA 1972-1992

At one point we did remodel to enclose a walkway that was already attached to the garage with a roof. This enabled us to move the laundry out of the east end of the kitchen giving us more space. We had a nice lawn in the back and one summer added a spa. My wife insists that she and Bruce dug the hole, but I remember helping some. She says I have a bad memory! What we did agree on was that the dirt we removed looked like a pile twice the size of the hole. And we had no idea how to get rid of the dirt.

Once when I was away, a good friend, John Kershaw, brought in a crew of young men and they used wheelbarrows and trucked it all away in a short time. What a blessing! John also gave us good advice on how to form the area around the spa with small stones imbedded in concrete so it wouldn't be slippery. Like many people we used the spa a lot after installation, but not as much later on. But our children, and later on our grandchildren, loved this feature of our place. Since both our children grew up, graduated from high school, got married and left home from this residence we have many family memories based on that location.

As bishop of the Midwest and Pacific conferences upon arriving in Upland in 1972 and being versed by Arthur Climenhaga, my predecessor, I spent some time learning to know pastors and churches in the whole area west of the Mississippi River. In the Pacific Conference I worked out of my home and office except for the churches in central California and Oregon. When visiting those churches and in the Midwest I usually stayed in the homes of the pastors and spouses. This was not always convenient but it certainly gave me insight into pastoral families and churches. It also saved on my expense account with the denomination.

When I became bishop of the Midwest and Pacific Conferences it was pretty much decided by precedent that I should have my office in Upland, California. My first office in 1972 consisted of two small rooms in the recently constructed Upland Manor, an apartment for seniors. It was a good arrangement. My secretary had a room and I had an adjoining room. During those first years, Donna Eyer, and later Joyce Ginder served well as my secretaries. The work assigned to a secretary was heavy when I was home and sparse when on the road.

Eventually the Upland Manor wanted the rooms. Ray Musser, then manager of our church financial foundation, and I worked on a plan to share offices in downtown Upland just north of the Christian Light Bookstore. Ray Musser had offices for the Jacob Engle Foundation, which he was willing to share with me. He had his own business office just across and up the street on the next block.

I had an office and a place for a secretary. During the years at this office in old town Upland, our daughter Bernice, Marilyn Harmon, Pauline Hanna and Eleanor Lehman served as secretaries. At some point in time Ray Musser felt they needed more room so the Jacob Engle Foundation and the bishop's office were moved to new office suites on Foothill Boulevard just east of Euclid Avenue. Noreen Villiceno served as my secretary there until the denomination built facilities in Pennsylvania in 1992. So since I was General Secretary, I was asked to move east.

All of the above secretaries were very patient with me and my schedule. They came with varying degrees of experience and skills. Noreen was the best trained and most experienced and took a dramatic reduction in pay to serve the church in this way. Joyce Ginder had served as secretary for Bishop Charlie Byers so she brought a wealth of skill and familiarity with church work in the earlier days of my experience as bishop.

Our daughter played a unique role in being a recent graduate of a business school. She was very professional, but when no one could see or hear she would quickly switch her role to our loving daughter. I must say we likely related better at work than at home. She was in her dating days and, as a parent, I decided I had to respond differently as her father than her boss as bishop.

At General Conference one year a pastor approached me and asked if, as a bishop, I could still accept a joke. I assured him I would always enjoy humor. At that point he patted me on the tummy and started laughing. In a few seconds I had the flashback of years before when the pastor's wife surprised me in the bathroom. I now knew the story was out. He said her husband told him. So I sought out her husband and told him I never divulged the names. But I did tell him in all my travels, his wife was especially kind. He could now laugh at the episode.

Chapter 16

Staying with Pastors

Staying in homes of pastors brought about some unique times and has left me with stories. I share those times before telling about the goals and core of my responsibilities as bishop.

On one of my first trips into the Midwest I was informed by one of the older pastors that I was not their choice for bishop. I accepted his statement but both he and I knew we had to make the best of it. The fact that I had married Marlene, who was born and raised near Abilene, Kansas, gave me a bit of credibility in the Midwest. But my youth (I was only 36 years old) and my theology and practice gave some pastors big question marks. I had been described by my bishop, Henry Ginder, as a pastor who had a conservative theology but a liberal practice. For example, I am a committed evangelical believer with my values squarely with the Brethren in Christ. But I would wear a maroon suit, bright ties and engage in sports events and owned a motorcycle. I also used humor frequently in the pulpit and at that point in time our church culture was more reserved in many of our congregations.

At any rate, after staying in the homes of the pastors, loving, laughing and praying with them, I felt accepted and we got on with business.

One incident, on moving west, was visiting in the home of Sam and Charlotte Hollingsworth. At the time he was pastor of the Colorado Springs Brethren in Christ church in 1972. He informed me he didn't need a bishop and I wouldn't need to visit him.

However, I informed him he may not need me, but I needed him and I wanted to learn to know the church there. So he reluctantly accepted my insistence to visit. They had five small children and after my first visit, he told me any one who could love and relate to his kids as I had done might just make a good bishop.

We became really good friends over the years ahead. I was usually hosted in their fairly small parsonage in a room on the lower level. His children enjoyed checking out the contents of my suitcase, especially my travel alarm clock. One morning I arose early to shave and shower. I heard a rap on the bathroom door and three of the younger children asked if they could watch me shave. I accommodated them, but their father finally hearing them came and chased them out. On that first visit the youngest child was still a baby and vomited all over me as I offered to hold him at a picnic and I was headed to the airport. In spite of washing off in a creek, the person sitting next to me in the plane seemed to react to the odor I still had on my arm and clothes. It was just being a bishop!

Several years later I was visiting in the home of Ron and Marilyn Freeman who had just been invited to our Rosebank church near Hope, Kansas. They were temporarily housed in a small rental house. They insisted I take their bedroom, even though they had three small girls all under the age of eight. They said they would be just fine out in the living room rollout bed. Sometime in the wee hours of the morning I awoke to what I thought might be a cat's tail on my forehead. I slowly reached for my small flashlight and discovered it was their middle daughter with a rag doll who apparently came to join her parents in bed. I heard her deep breathing as she drifted off into a deep sleep. I covered her and then waited for dawn.

Early in the morning I heard Ron working in the small bathroom that had a slow drain. I heard him groan and say "Oh no!" I learned later the whole drain had fallen out.

Then his wife Marilyn asked where he had put Veronica, the little girl who was now in bed with me. He said, "She is still in the rollout bed." There was a long silence and then I spoke and said, "Come and get her." Ron came in, but she held my head firmly and wanted her mommy. Marilyn reluctantly came and got her. Ron, at breakfast, said he was going to print in their church bulletin that the first time the bishop visited I slept with their daughter.

He, of course, was joking. But it could have ruined my reputation since he was not known in our denomination, nor was the age of his daughter. The little four-year old girl was embarrassed but I'll relate a story later when she turned the tables on me when she became a teenager.

Ironically, the most traditional and conservative congregation I would visit in the Midwest decided to employ a young couple just out of seminary. I was reluctant to bless this match, but agreed. I'll never forget when the pastor met me at the airport in cutoff jeans and a tank top. I groaned inwardly knowing what I would likely face with the church board. I was surprised when the church board complained about his wife wearing *hot pants* which I would have called shorts, but so it went. They didn't even mention the pastor's attire, which I thought would be a big issue. As I recall the members of the church board at that time were all women. I was still learning!

This same couple had a dog that was very dear to them. On one of my visits someone in the neighborhood had put out poison, likely for another dog, but it made their dog very ill. The dog was having seizures upon my arrival. We took the dog across the city to a veterinarian while I held their young son in the back seat. The pastor, at one point, looked in the rear view mirror and commented to his wife that the bishop sure gets involved in duties that have nothing to do with his training. I had to admit he was right! The dog had to be "put down" that weekend so it was a dramatic time for all involved. Years later we could all reminisce about such incidents.

The following are more stories of my relationships with pastors. Some are humorous and others reveal the pathos of life. The stories are not in chronological order, just random recollections of some of the more memorable times.

One family with whom I related to across two conferences and still keep in touch with today is Kevin and Gail Ryan and their three children. Our journey began when I called them to pastor the Zion Brethren in Christ church near Abilene, Kansas. Kevin had come out of city life in New Jersey, and Gail had been raised in the quiet college town of Carlisle, Pennsylvania. They brought together two cultures and a variety of values and family practices. Their great strength was their love for each other and their open confrontation.

On one of my first visits with them in Kansas we were up talking late into the night. We decided to retire for the night. I had just gotten into my pajamas when I heard Gail scream from the kitchen. Kevin and I both rushed out to find the kitchen and dining area covered with water. The spray hose at the kitchen sink had popped off. Kevin finally found a place to shut the water off and then we spent a long time mopping up water with towels and mops. It was well after midnight when we finished. It was a "bonding" experience.

Kevin loved the quiet countryside and enjoyed the rural culture of Kansas. Gail missed the urban college community life where she had grown up, but they both adjusted and served the congregation well. After years there I called them to lead a church planting in Chino Hills, California. At first it went very well, but as time passed Kevin discerned that church planting was not his greatest strength.

During the years in California, I would often play golf with Kevin and we would have breakfast frequently. One morning I met him and I saw right away he was very depressed. I inquired what was up. He responded that his life was over. He then shared that Gail was expecting their third child and they could not handle this unexpected outcome. Well, we talked and I encouraged Kevin to continue and they would be able to deal with it. Later on the couple came to see their third child, a son they named Michael, as a great blessing.

When they left California they moved to Souderton, Pennsylvania, where they had a good long run with Kevin as pastor of one of our larger churches. Kevin and Gail were just one of those compatible couples with Marlene and me. We have continued contacts, which have enriched our friendship over the years.

In the Midwest conference, I wrote before that my wife Marlene, who was born and raised near Abilene, Kansas, was a factor that gave me some credibility and trust with pastors who might have been suspicious of me as a person. My theology and practice was different than most of the pastors in that conference at the time. But we came to love them in many ways. Henry Landis was instrumental in seeing that Marlene had her way provided to attend the annual pastors and spouses retreats which were a highlight of each year for me. Marlene has a way of being direct and honest that seems to always appeal to pastors and wives.

One of the older couples, Henry and Faithe Landis, often hosted me in their home. Our journey started in Oklahoma, then to Pharr, Texas, and then Abilene, Kansas. On one occasion, in Oklahoma, on one of my first visits I was rocking in a large lounge chair when it suddenly toppled over backwards, and I flipped head over heels flailing arms and legs to try to catch myself. Any dignity I had as a bishop was all gone. We all had a hearty laugh.

Pastor Henry Landis and Bishop Don

Another couple in the Abilene area that was always a joy to me was Charles and Elaine Norman who had a long tenure at the Rosebank Brethren in Christ church near Hope, Kansas. Charles was known to play pranks. He and his wife conspired to see if they could catch me in one. Charles had a tape of a wild charismatic service and he had dubbed in his announcement and related to me that it was a service that one of his members insisted on having held at Rosebank.

Now it would be an understatement to say Charles was not given to loud charismatic worship services, but rather orderly services. For example, he had often filled in as pastor for a Presbyterian church not far from them. He and Elaine played the tape and Charles would note how one of their most composed deacons had shouted. As I listened in total disbelief, Elaine finally said, "Charles, this isn't right." I caught on and he was so disappointed that his wife had broken the prank. It confirmed my opinion that Elaine was a woman of grace. Charles was capable of being gracious himself but it was more fun for him to engage in creative humor. He had told me how he once put cereal in a dog food box and ate it as an evening snack in front of an evangelist who was staying in their home. The man watched in horror, refused to share the biscuits (cereal) and of course told the story far and wide. Charles is still laughing about it.

I often talked with their son, Stanley, and he later entered our ministry team and became a pastor. In fact he is now pastor of a cowboy church—a fitting and novel idea for the Midwest. He seems to flourish in this role.

Charles and Elaine were bi-vocational and also ran a memorial stone business in Abilene. Charles regaled me with stories of selling memorial stones and strange events resulting in side splitting laughs. Charles also had a pilot's license. Once he flew me in his small aircraft from Wichita, Kansas to Abilene, Kansas. As we flew north we passed a nearby thunderstorm that gave me some apprehension. I asked Charles if lightning ever struck planes and he told me it was not supposed to. It was not a comfort to me.

One tragic event happened when Ed and Deanna Rickman were assigned as pastor and wife at the Abilene Brethren in Christ church. Deanna had a brain hemorrhage and died suddenly, leaving Ed with three young children. I immediately flew to Abilene and spent hours with him. The two of us went to the funeral home and Ed poured out his broken heart in grief. Then the two of us drove back to Abilene after the funeral and interment in Iowa. It was a learning experience in dealing with grief and in observing a young man and father having to face death and the future.

He eventually married his second wife, Martha, who became a very good wife and mother to his children. They later moved to Canada to pastor a church and, subsequent to the Canadian experience, he became president of Vennard College in Iowa. Our paths have crossed numerous times across the years.

One story that involved Henry Landis, Charles Norman and Ed Rickman was a trip I made after having had dental surgery. During the flight from California to Kansas I had experienced extreme pain and the airline hostess had given me a number of aspirin. She thought I had taken enough aspirin, so she then offered some brandy to rinse my mouth hoping it would help. When Henry Landis picked me up in Wichita he evidently smelled the brandy and asked if I was on medication. I told him the story and he had a hearty laugh.

That night at a men's banquet at the Abilene church, I sat by a guest Baptist minister who was the speaker. I kept popping aspirin and he must have smelled my breath, so I guessed he might have concluded the Brethren in Christ Bishop of the Midwest was an addict of alcohol and drugs.

After the meeting, Charles and Ed asked me how I was coping with my toothache. I quickly confessed my intense pain. It was getting late, sometime after 10 p.m., when Charles called a dentist friend in Salina, Kansas. Charles and Henry took me there where he uncapped a tooth on which I had a root canal. The dentist then explained the air pressure changes that occurred while flying had likely induced great pain. He gave me some pain pills and I was able to sleep peacefully without pain. The dentist was a kind man and I was glad Charles Norman had him as a friend.

During the time Charles and Barbara Rickel functioned as the pastor and wife at Bethany, Oklahoma they hosted regional Conference one year. Bob Hempy, pastor of my home church at Upland, California, and I were staying in the Rickel home. Barbara had told me on the side that she was fixing "calf fries" in the scrambled eggs for breakfast. She wondered if that would be acceptable. Of course I thought it was great.

As we were eating, Bob Hempy's curiosity finally got him to gingerly inquire if it was sausage in the eggs. Barbara blushed and said, "Not really" and glanced at me. I told Bob they were "rocky mountain oysters." He looked puzzled and I said, "Well, it is part of a beef that you would never find on a cow." He paused, looked at me incredulously and asked if I was serious. I assured him I was and had told Barbara to serve them. He declined a second helping. I was filled with laughter and asked for seconds.

Along the same line, I went out to a restaurant with Jim and Gladys Esh when he was pastor in Colorado Springs. I saw they had "rocky mountain oysters" on the menu. I asked Jim and Gladys to keep a straight face. I told the waitress I was from California and I wondered what kind of oysters these were and which ocean they came from. She looked at Jim and Gladys and they broke a smile and then she said, "It doesn't matter sir, you need to eat them." We all had a good laugh.

Marlene was often a topic of conversation since I was often lonely for her and pastoral couples were interested in how we coped with my being away from home. One incident that proved to be a memorable topic of conversation was when Marlene would sort my socks after laundry. I wore almost all dark blue or black socks. Once I mentioned they weren't properly matched, so she sewed little colorful bits of yarn to make them match. When I would remove my shoes in the homes of pastors and spouses, I would be asked what the colorful yarn spots were. I called them Marlene's designer socks. I then explained what the purpose was and it always ended in a good laugh and I might add an appreciation for my wife's ingenuity.

Chapter 17

Church Planting

"A time to plant" (Eccl. 3:2)

During 1972 through 1974, I visited all of the churches in the Midwest and Pacific Conferences. I sensed now that I had some knowledge and relationship with the pastors. I set about to discern what would be my calling and purpose as a bishop.

One of the events I planned in the Pacific Conference was to invite pastors and other church leaders to Mile High Pines (a church camp for the Pacific Regional Conference). I inquired of them what they would like to see happen in the Pacific conference in the next five to ten years. What I heard could be summarized by saying, "whatever you do, don't begin anything new." Well, these were discouraging words to me. Actually I was hoping to hear them say, start new churches. So I asked the Lord what he wanted and words of Scripture came to me about, "I am making everything new." (Rev. 21:5) or "People are to become new creatures in Christ Jesus" (Col. 6:15). I was moved and motivated to challenge and lead the conferences in something new.

I realized that they thought a church planting, which they had done some fifteen years before, was too costly, and was not a success. But I had a vision that was really different than the model of the 1950's. At that time our denomination would build a new church facility, employ a pastor and begin a church. I proposed that church plantings should be focused on people rather than a building. I wanted to change their poor memory to an exciting mission.

In the fall of 1974, I enrolled at the Fuller Theological Seminary in Pasadena, California. It was the first year for the Seminary, along with their School of World Missions, to offer a Doctorate in Ministry program. I decided on church planting as a major. The Brethren in Christ had not started any new churches in over a decade in the Pacific conference and I was convinced that both the Midwest and Pacific conferences could reach new people and experience growth if they planted churches. So the balance of my years as bishop, from 1974-1985, were invested in both the care of pastors and in starting new churches.

My time at Fuller Seminary resulted in my meeting John Wimber, who had been starting new churches for the Quakers. He was also at the very beginning of forming the Vineyard Movement, a new denomination of what I would describe as an arm of the charismatic movement. Aaron Stern, who was then pastor of the Ontario Brethren in Christ church, and I were both taking the same courses. During one class project, we visited Pastor Robert Schuller in his office and listened to his story of starting the Garden Grove Community Church.

Aaron and I sat with John Wimber in the sanctuary of the Garden Grove Community church (the former facility adjacent to what is now known as the Crystal Cathedral), which we were visiting as a class at that time. I asked John Wimber if we could hire him as a consultant. He agreed and when I asked him about the cost, he mentioned $5,000. I must have looked like I was in shock. He then said, "Since Aaron and you are studying at Fuller Seminary and have your heads screwed on straight about church growth, I will reduce it to $3,000." I took this proposal of hiring John Wimber to the Pacific Conference boards and they surprised me by agreeing to employ John.

It was the beginning of an adventure. John asked me to get two other couples together. Marlene and I chose Aaron and Martha Stern, and Glenn and Joyce Ginder. I should add that Gordon and Eunice Engle would replace Glenn and Joyce when they moved to Oregon.

We met monthly with John Wimber for a year. The late John Wimber was a man who enabled me to build vision and challenge the status quo. I recall him advising me to trust God, but watch out for some of his people. It was part humor but also part of reality. He spent many hours with Marlene and me along with the persons named above as our Pacific Conference Church Planting Team. These people were supporters, analyzers, helpers, and correctors in the challenge to plant ten churches in ten years in the Pacific Regional Conference.

After some training we launched our first church plant in Alta Loma, California. For the first planting we started two home Bible studies and they were both going well. Gordon and Eunice Engle sold their residence in Upland and moved to Alta Loma to help plan Bible Studies for the new church. This couple really was committed to help with church planting. Then we invited Ralph and Joan Wenger, from Paramount, Maryland to come and pastor this first church plant. Ralph was one of the few persons to pioneer church planting in our denomination. It went very well. And now some thirty years later it is one of the largest Brethren in Christ congregations in the Pacific Conference. Of course that is the best story. We did plant over ten churches in the Pacific Conference over the next ten years, but some of them failed. But John Wimber's advice to us was that it is better to start numerous churches and have some fail than not start any at all.

In the Midwest Conference I did not have a team but I really appreciated the regional conference board along with Charles and Elaine Norman and Warren and Connie Hoffman who helped us launch into the cities of Wichita, Kansas and Oklahoma City, Oklahoma. The Bethany congregation and their pastor at the time, Charles Rickel, were very helpful in the Oklahoma City launch. Another couple that helped with the Oklahoma planting was my sister in law and her husband, Ernestine and Ira Eyster.

I should point out that Ralph and Joan Wenger had successfully planted a new church near Hagerstown, Maryland. Joan wanted to know if they came to California if she could live in a semi-rural area. I told her there were building lots large enough in the area to accommodate horses. Little did I know that the area would be filled with houses in a heavy populated area within a few short years after their arrival. Joan has often smiled about that development.

One of the new moves I made was encouraging and employing new young pastors. Many of them came from other traditions. I was both blest and criticized for these choices. I might also add that some of these pastors failed. But a number of them became strong church leaders. I never regretted taking a risk with committed pastors.

Sometime in late 2002, a good friend of mine, John Kershaw, was approached by a church member who questioned the church planting efforts in the Pacific Conference during 1974-1984. The following is a statement I wrote in the summer of 2003 as a response to John Kershaw since he requested it in writing.

Greetings John:

First, thank you for asking about Church Planting in the Pacific Conference of the Brethren in Christ. I was intrigued and challenged by reviewing the history of church planting in which I was involved. My observations cover the years of 1975-1984 when I was serving as bishop of the Pacific Conference.

It is significant that the Pacific Conference had not planted any new churches between 1954 and 1972 when I came to the conference. Therefore, there was a need for some new vision and a plan to share the faith in our area, by way of our congregations. It would be of interest to also note the membership in the Pacific Conference was between 900 and 960 members from 1964 to 1972. When we started church planting in 1974 it started a new growth pattern and rate, so by the year 2000 we were over 1,500 members.

As you noted, there were ten churches planted during the years 1976 and 1984. All but three of those did not continue. However, Alta Loma was the first one started in

1976 and is now one of the largest congregations in the Pacific Conference.

An honest question you raised is, "What were the factors in the growth or lack of growth of these new churches?" As I reflected on that question, it is obvious that there were numerous factors.

In my judgment **the most crucial factor were the pastors of those churches.** If the pastor had experience, **a sense of call** that this was a mandate from God, **and a plan for growth**, the church tended to not only survive but grow.

Another major issue was my **leadership style.** I was fairly young (36 years old in 1972) and daring (you could call it faith) but I decided to take risks! I believed it was better to start ten new churches in ten years than not start any. I also chose some young and inexperienced pastors, some without adequate training, but they wanted an opportunity to start a new church and I took some calculated risks.

As a matter of fact, our consultant (the late John Wimber who started "The Vineyard" movement) advised me it would be **better to try and fail, than not to try, so do something new.** I believed that was sound and Biblical advice.

Another major factor was the **Bible Study groups** that formed the nucleus of these church plantings. The strongest and best church planting was the foundation of the Alta Loma church. We had two strong Bible Studies before the church was opened. We also called the most experienced pastor.

Factors involved in church plantings that failed were unexpected issues such as illness, marriage problems, or discouragement of the church planting pastors. We have since learned that it takes a **uniquely qualified pastor to plant a church**. Since 1984, we and other denominations now screen and train church planting pastors before *assignment. We did not have that process in the years we started new churches.*

Another note of some significance, I was in the first class of the Fuller Theological Seminary Doctor of Ministry track where the whole church growth movement started with Donald McGavern and Peter Wagner. I can honestly tell you these were exciting years for me. As I reflect back, I'm glad that we took the risks.

We also discussed the issue of money. As I told you, we raised enough money the first year in one evening that tripled the annual budget of the Pacific Conference Board of Extension at that time. Over the next seven or eight years we began annual fund drives which enabled us to receive between $25,000 and $55,000 annually which was income to assist many of the new congregational budgets. Our plan was for the new churches to raise their own funds. We helped to subsidize operations over a three to five year reduction plan.

One other factor we did not discuss was the attention given to existing churches. I spoke often with existing church pastors and urged them to have a vision for giving and growing. The Upland Brethren in Christ church had a good growth period during 1974-1984 and the churches in Moreno Valley were also motivated to new growth and went from part time to full time churches. The Ontario church went off subsidy, which it had been receiving for over fifteen years.

This is certainly not the whole story, but it does represent my response and reflection about the church planting years when I was bishop. I would rather have tried what we did than not to have tried. There are more people actively involved in building the Kingdom of God now than before we tried these efforts of church planting not only in the Pacific Conference but across the denomination.

And in conclusion, let me report on an event last Sunday. I was at the Riverside Brethren in Christ church on Sunday, June 1, 2003. It was my privilege to speak on behalf of the bishop and the Pacific Conference in blessing a new church planting called Crest Community, which comes out of the Riverside Brethren. So the seeds of growth continue to be planted and take root. Some will grow and some will not, but I believe it is better to keep on planting!

Chapter 18

Adventures in Maturing

"A season for every activity under heaven" (Eccl. 3:1)

I might note here that during these years of 1972-1984, when I was bishop, there were some events forever etched in our memories.

Our two children grew up and became high school seniors before I realized time was so fleeting. Bernice graduated from high school on June 14th, 1977. And her brother Bruce graduated three years later in the spring of 1980. In the meantime I went back to school and received a Doctor of Ministry degree on June 9th, 1979 from Fuller Theological Seminary.

Shafer family 1976

Bernice met a young man at high school, Robert Worley. Bob, as we knew him, had already graduated and then returned to Upland High School to help with some of the drama. He and Bernice became romantically involved.

Since Bob was four years older and we didn't know him, we were concerned. Bernice assured us he was a good man. But parents are always protective and I was really not sure about this relationship. Bob would visit the house and we got to know him. Then after Bernice's graduation we encouraged her to attend Messiah College in Grantham, Pennsylvania. As a dad, I was secretly hoping she would meet a fine young Christian man. But instead Bob pursued the relationship and even skipped meals to save money so he could travel east to see his beloved Bernice.

Since I wasn't home many weekends, Bob would come to visit Marlene while Bernice was away at school. On one occasion Marlene went to the back bedroom and didn't answer the door. I told her that seemed rather cold. But then when I came home she had invited him for a meal! I tried to tell her not to feed him since that would only give him incentive to come more often.

We were encouraged when Bob would attend the Upland church with Bernice and one Easter he made a commitment to follow Christ. During that time, we had a guest, John Graybill (a missionary to Japan I mention later), visit us. He had some private time with Bernice. He asked if her fiancé had joined the church. She told him he had not at that time. He then related a story about how young men sometimes make great promises and then change after a wedding. Bernice asked him some questions and he strongly urged her to have Bob make a commitment to the local church. All we knew was that a few months later Bob decided to join the Upland church.

I thought John Graybill's sharing with Bernice would boomerang and I would be accused of telling him to talk to her. But I was wrong. Bernice never said a word about her conversation with John Graybill. Bernice and Bob did pre-marital counseling with Pastor Bob Hempy and he informed me they were quite compatible and I was the one seeming to have an issue. I wanted to tell him to get lost, but I held my tongue. To make a longer story short, they were married on June 21, 1980. I was honored to perform the wedding ceremony of our beloved daughter and her husband Bob who has blest our family.

Bernice and Bob's Wedding, 1980

One morning in the spring of 1983, I was attending a committee meeting in an Upland restaurant when I received a phone call. My brother, Sam, called and informed me that our dad suddenly had a heart attack and died. It was March 14th. It was a horrible shock. Dad was only 67 and I felt the loss keenly. I went back to the committee, told them the news, and excused myself. One man asked me if I couldn't finish the meeting. I politely told him I had to leave. I just wanted to be alone and then share my grief with my wife and family. It was a very hard time and I recall I came down with a severe cold.

I carried out my duties, led a Midwest Regional Conference session, and a pastors and spouses retreat. Then Marlene and I headed back east for the funeral and memorial service.

After the funeral service my mother asked my brother, Sam, and me to sort through dad's desk. We came across a number of invoices my dad had never turned in. My brother told me he knew dad was doing this. Dad would let some men get by when they wouldn't pay, but my brother was more business-like.

I asked him what he was going to do. He sat there for a bit, and then tore up the invoices. I said, well some of dad's generous spirit rubbed off. He then told me the day of grace was over for those who weren't paying.

Many of dad's customers came to his viewing and I knew my dad was a much appreciated man not only by his wife and family, but by many others. My brother was standing near me and would point out many who owed the auto parts store a lot of money. He looked at me and said, "They will not be at my viewing."

I would find myself weeping driving alone when the reality of dad's death settled in on me. I have missed him over the years since. My mother carried on quite well.

Back in California, our son, Bruce, had graduated from California Polytechnic University and he and his girlfriend, Carol, planned their wedding. Again I was honored to share in their wedding ceremony. They informed me they were writing their own vows. I might note that as we were planning, I said that in the ceremony I would pronounce them "man and wife." Carol quickly responded that would not be acceptable. She helped me realize I had used the word "man" instead of "husband." She was absolutely correct. I had made a slip. But I also understood our son was marrying a woman as strong as my wife.

They had a lovely wedding in the Webb Chapel in Claremont, California on March 30, 1985. At their wedding reception, pie was served instead of cake which suited me just fine. We were now a family of six. And Carol has also blest our family. She is very talented and in recent years has taught art in their local high school.

Carol and Bruce's Wedding, 1985

Chapter 19

Other Cultures

When I became a bishop in 1972 I was launched into some cross-cultural experiences in our own country. At least, I am convinced they are cross-cultural experiences.

The one experience was in San Francisco, California where we had a ministry called Life Line Mission. For many years it was a skid row ministry where we held services and then served meals to many people off the streets. As you may guess, there were all types of people and many of them not sober. Some actually made decisions to change their lifestyle and became very reliable citizens and functional members in churches and communities.

I knew of one man, an alcoholic, who had accepted Jesus and became a Christian. He married a volunteer and in later years was a pastor of a small church.

On the other hand, I knew a man, who was a con artist with several names, who eventually married a young woman volunteer and he later killed her. So it was life in the extremes.

I met persons who were transsexual, transvestites, drunks, prostitutes and people who came from a way of life vastly different than the quiet little town in Pennsylvania from where I had come.

Later this city mission was changed to help single, homeless women, and mothers. Eventually the ministry was moved out of San Francisco to Upland, California where it still operates. It is now called Pacific Lifeline, a ministry that successfully helps women and their children get a new start on life.

A second involvement was with a mission in Farmington, New Mexico with the Navajo Indian culture. Wilmer Heisey introduced me to this mission. For many years we had a hospital, school and chapel. We also had a well drilled for water that has served the Navajo community for many years. Then the government helped with schools and medical issues. So in later years we added a gym and laundry facilities to serve the community.

Marion Heisey came later and he started the vision to help recovering alcoholics. The mission now has such a program.

Ben and Eunice Stoner have lived in the Navajo community for many years and learned the language. They have identified with the Navajo people and helped many families find faith in Jesus and become stable members of the community. I have been told that this culture is one of the most difficult for people to understand. No doubt our history with Native Americans has a lot to do with these issues.

I served on the Board of Directors for both these missions when I was bishop. Later we had our Board for World Missions involved in these cross-culture arenas.

In 1979, Roy Sider, former colleague as bishop, became the Executive Director of World Missions, and he invited Marlene and me to visit the Brethren in Christ churches in Japan and India. It was quite an experience. We flew to Tokyo, Japan via a stop in Hawaii. We were hosted in Japan by John and Lucille Kraybill and had contacts with Marlin and Ruth Zook. I was excited to see the house churches in Japan.

One side experience was the time John Kraybill took Marlene and me to the public baths. John told Marlene a man would be sitting at the top of a wall that separated the genders, but he would be watching both the men and women bathe. As it turned out it was a female that evening, a rare change, so the laugh was on John. John explained to me that while in America we wash feet (a practice in our Anabaptist churches), but in Japan the men wash each other's backs and then sit in very hot water.

It was also memorable to travel on the *bullet train* to our churches in southern Japan. John hosted us with a church leader to a special taste of "sake," a warm rice wine. That night when he introduced me, he said I had learned thirteen Japanese words, and then named their cities and with heavily accented English words, like "fust base, sukond base, thud base, etcetera." When I got up, I said he forgot the word "sake." The people laughed and John turned very red!

Then we flew to India by way of Hong Kong. Our experience in Calcutta where we landed at the "Dum Dum Airport" was dramatic. The two men who were to meet us somehow had been informed we were flying in from Bombay and that flight had been cancelled. We were feeling isolated and lost in the airport late at night. In an effort to get some communication going, I had to leave Marlene alone with the luggage. A number of Indian men surrounded us after I had exchanged our money for rupees and the rate of exchange made us look very wealthy.

I was taken in behind the counter and she was alone. She was really terrified, but after some time we finally reached the men by phone and they took us to the Mennonite Central Committee offices and our place of lodging.

The next day J. N. Gosh and Heim Paul took us through the city of Calcutta. We visited Mother Teresa's hospitals for babies and for the dying. It was like walking on holy ground. We shall never forget the sisters carrying babies or just rubbing their backs and there was no crying or chaos, just peace. There was also a holy hush in the hospital for the dying where Mother Teresa wanted people to experience love before they left this world.

We hosted the two Indian men to an Indian lunch and they took us to an immaculate restaurant. The cleanliness on the inside of Mother Teresa's hospitals and the restaurant was in stark contrast to the filth of the streets.

We also did some shopping. Marlene enjoyed the bartering, but I was so struck with the poverty. I just wanted to pay what they asked and get back to our travels. One little beggar girl caught my eye and I really wanted to give her something but the Indian men advised against it lest there be fifteen to twenty children begging from us. It pained me to not give her a gift, but I heeded their advice.

Overnight we traveled by train north to the state of Bihar. At one point Marlene went to the ladies room. Heim Paul asked where my wife was and I informed him. He quickly took me to the restroom and knocked and when he was sure she was fine, he then advised me to never leave her alone since white women often disappeared on the trains! We stayed very close the rest of the trip!

The poverty in some parts of India is indescribable. Yet the gracious people and their hospitality were unrivaled. Marlene struggled with some of their cuisine. When we were served chicken, there were parts on the plate she was not accustomed to seeing, yet alone eating. I advised her to not look, just eat. But she did some discreet gagging. John and Ethel Sider, who were with us, helped her by eating her portions on some occasions.

We did enjoy their goat stew which was prepared outdoors in a huge pot for a large crowd. The goat was slaughtered early in the morning just outside the house where we were staying. I awoke Marlene and told her to view the beginning of our noon meal. She was not thrilled to say the least.

We were also honored to attend a funeral of an esteemed church leader, known as Benjamin, while we were visiting. It was conducted late at night and we were invited to help with the burial as many put dirt on the grave.

We were able to stop briefly in Europe and visited Switzerland and then on to Amsterdam where Marlene's niece, Peggy, lived. The prostitution in Amsterdam is known throughout the world. As we walked down the street, we saw women in storefronts and on the street wearing very scanty lingerie. Marlene advised me to keep looking straight ahead. I did my best, but I am a curious man. Marlene's niece was away but we stayed in their apartment and learned of the ministry they were in to help mothers and other women escape the downgrading life of prostitution.

Then we crossed the English Channel by ship and had a couple of days in London. We were hosted by former school friends, Charlie and Miriam Byers. They gave us a really great tour of the city. Charlie also took us to visit a pub to show how families gather socially in Wimbledon where they lived. We returned to California via New York and the memories of those times changed our lives forever. I gave talks on church growth in Japan and India, but I felt I learned far more than any teaching or sharing I gave. Marlene and I were blest by this adventure.

During 1984 through 1996 I attended Mennonite World Conferences in France, Paraguay, Canada and the United States. Perhaps the most memorable conference was the event in Paraguay up on a high desert, often referred to as the "green hell." Mennonites had migrated there years before from Europe and some by way of Canada. Most of them spoke German or Spanish. I was hosted in a private home and had a roommate from Columbia, South America. Our hostess spoke just a bit of English but most of the conversation was in German or Spanish.

One afternoon I was reading when my roommate suddenly shut the shutters, turned out the light, and stretched out on the bed. I sat in the dark and then realized it was their custom to take a nap mid-afternoon. I decided to try to fit in with the pattern. The next day I was due back at the church, but I noticed my hosts were packing a picnic basket. I guessed they would drop me off, but instead they took me in a different direction and I missed the meeting. But I enjoyed tasting their matte tea and seeing wild life in the high desert. They laughed at me trying to fit in and gave me the very strong tea, which I politely said was "interesting"—it was strong enough to knock an ox on his rump! They of course had set me up. Their laughter at my expense was rewarding.

On another trip I traveled with Harvey Sider to Manila in the Philippines for an Evangelism Conference. It was intriguing to see the culture there and the success of the Christian Missionary Alliance planting numerous churches in that setting.

In 1992 the Mennonite Central Committee sent a delegation of twelve of us to visit the Middle East. We were in Jordan, Syria, Egypt, Israel and Palestine.

A very interesting contact in Jordan was a visit to the brother of President Hussein. He was head of the Jordan military and was married to a woman from the United States who had been a Quaker. He was extremely intelligent and spoke at least three languages. We had been informed he was a Muslim and so one of our group asked him about his understanding of Christianity. He said, "Well, Jesus grew up just a few miles down the road so we are quite familiar with his teachings." It brought a smile to all of us.

One memorable moment was one morning when Jim Holms, my roommate, and I took an early morning walk in Amman, Jordan. Suddenly we were confronted by a soldier bearing a high-powered rifle who ordered us to HALT! We did! He then, in broken English, informed us we had entered a military compound. We informed him we were totally unaware of entering the compound and he believed us. Neither of us had any identification; we were in sweat suits only! Instead of arresting or shooting us he warned us not to return to that area. We stayed closer to the hotel from then on!

When we entered Syria, Jim Holms had a stamp in his passport that he had been to Israel so they wouldn't let him enter the country. He had to return to the hotel in Jordan. He would later join us in Egypt. Syria was a spooky country and we were told not to mention the word "Israel" or we could be deported instantly. We were advised to refer to Israel as "Disneyland."

The monks in Syria were most gracious and hosted us to a sumptuous meal. I enjoyed the variety of food and flavors in the Mideast but Marlene, who was not along, would not have enjoyed some of the pickled parts of animals that were served to us!

Later in the Cairo, Egypt airport I found myself left behind when an agent insisted my visa was not current. So I had to go to a bank window to purchase a new one and, when I returned the group was gone! It was late at night when I made my way to the parking area. There was very meager lighting and I could not spot the van in which we were traveling. The eleven had gone on. I heard later they were talking in the van and someone asked how I felt. When there was silence, they discovered I was not there!

They returned and finally found me wandering in and out of the airport. It improved my prayer life! I was very frustrated not being able to converse with anyone and trying to find the group in and out of the airport. I must say I was most affirmed that they were able to go on without missing me since I am not known to be "the quiet type."

A memory that stays with me was a meeting of Jews and Arabs in an upper room in Palestine where they shared deep feelings about the hatred of centuries between Jews and Arabs but agreed to dialogue in peace. It was a meeting called "rapprochement" or reconciliation in an upper room. I remember it was very cold and my feet were telling me they were nearly frostbitten, but I felt like taking off my shoes since it seemed we were on holy ground.

Another visit in Nazareth was to meet Father Chacour, an Arab by birth, a Jew by citizenship, and a Christian pastor. He reminded us of the pastor who once lived in Nazareth, a man called Jesus.

In Egypt we visited the pyramids and numerous churches there. It was an eye opener to observe Christians living in a hostile environment and, yet, their accent was on love.

Before Roy Sider left the missions office he had started the process of inviting Marlene and me to visit our churches in Zambia and Zimbabwe, Africa. It was also a memorable experience. I had heard of missions in Africa since I was a lad. Thus in 1993 we visited the historic churches and met people we had known. John and Eva Brubaker, our longtime friends from Nappanee, Indiana days, were now serving a short term in Zambia. They hosted us and we also met with Robert and Winnie Worman and Paul and Lela Hostettler who were at the Macha hospital and we had a great time with them. Together we visited the Hwange Game Preserve.

It was moving to see what world missions had accomplished across the years. When I asked why some of the mission stations were so far apart, they told me a story about Francis Davidson, an early missionary, who would move as far away as she could from new men who came as administrators from the United States or Canada since she didn't want them telling her how to do missions. My wife liked to hear her story! I was reminded of my dad's opinion that my wife was a strong woman!

We also connected with former college classmates, Jake and Nancy Shenk, who have, and are still spending most of their lives in Africa. They have a great grasp of the language and love the people and culture there.

Africa is a land of both beauty and poverty. The tribes and their ways have always been a challenge for the west. Our ways of doing missions had changed dramatically and the striving for independence from the colonization of former centuries has, and is, leaving scars and struggles for the present peoples of the two countries we visited. As in any society, there are persons with great strengths and love, and then there are those who take advantage for themselves at the expense of others. It is a process happening anywhere on the globe.

Chapter 20

Relaxing

"A time to keep and a time to throw away" (Eccl. 3:6)

In the early part of our marriage Marlene and I bought a Sears tent, 10 foot by 12 foot, with an exterior frame and sewed in floor. My wife would not risk any rodents crossing us in the night! (I discovered even before we were married, Marlene had no fear of insects or even snakes, but a mouse, dead or alive, terrorized her. She still has that fear which I think was implanted by three brothers on either side of her who had no mercy in this case.) We would go camping in many of the state parks of Pennsylvania. It was something we could afford and our children loved it.

I recall one of our early trips when we were eager to get going and once we arrived at the campsite, I discovered I forgot the exterior frame. What is a tent without poles? It was good for a sermon illustration, but at the time my wife and children looked at me as a dad who had lost his marbles. Fortunately we were not too far away, so I returned home alone to get the frame. My youngest sister, Nancy, was along and she didn't help my reputation with our children.

On another early outing with our tent I had found a really heavy canvas tarp I put under the tent to protect the tent floor. I used about three feet of it to serve as a *porch* so we didn't drag dirt into the tent. Well it worked great until I set up the tent in a nice gully down by a stream. A thunderstorm came up during the night and we found ourselves nearly floating on our air mattresses. The canvas *porch* also made a nice funnel to channel rain water right under the tent. So I learned to pitch the tent on higher ground and dig a little trench around the tent when it looked like rain.

We also met new people. One family in western Pennsylvania introduced us to "kielbasa," a polish sausage, which became a favorite item in our cooking for decades. In the southern part of the United States people introduced us to *dough boys* which is Bisquick wrapped around a stick which you toast over an open fire, then pull it off and fill with butter and honey or jelly. They taste so good on a cool night.

Once in Kentucky I was showing our son, Bruce, how to shave a stick, always pointing the blade away from you. He went off to play; I turned the blade toward me to shave off a small knot on the branch and quickly sliced into my thumb. Hours later I had stitches in my thumb and a large bandaged fist. In that southern doctor's office there was a large bulletin board displaying an unusual number and variety of fish lures with nasty looking hooks. Our son asked the doctor if he was a fisherman. The doctor, in a southern drawl, informed him he was an unusual fisherman, in that he fished those lures out of people's eyebrows, backs, arms, legs, ears, heads, and often rumps. The doctor had a great sense of humor and saved my thumb as well.

Back at our campsite our son asked how I cut myself, and I had to tell him to do what I say, not what I do. Many people think that is what pastors do too often. Ouch!

One year we shared a canoe trip down the Rappahannock River in Virginia with the Glenn Ginder family. The water was getting low near the end of the summer and we would sometimes hit rocks going through the rapids. At one point Glenn's canoe hit a hidden rock and their oldest daughter, Connie, was tossed out into the air and then into the fast moving river. Our son took it as really funny and wanted to experience the same thing. We had to explain it was an accident and very dangerous since she could have landed on a rock.

Speaking of danger, the next morning Connie came out of her tent on a cool morning, walked over to the fire pit and, not knowing how hot it can be under gray ashes, stepped into them and immediately blistered both of her bare feet. Her scream still sizzles in my mind. It was an extremely painful lesson.

On that particular trip Glenn, Bruce and I were in the men's room and a grandfather was getting a shave from a grandson. The commode lids in the men's room were painted with wild life. After commenting on the clean and unusual facilities, the old gentlemen asked whether we younger men and boys knew about "outhouses." Glenn and I assured him we had known about them, but our son Bruce had not. The older man then proceeded to quote the following poem that sent us into gales of laughter.

The Passing of the Backhouse

When memory keeps me company and moves to smiles
    and tears,
a weather beaten object looms through the mist of
    years.
Behind the house and barn it stood a half a mile or
    more
and hurrying feet a path had made, straight to its
    swinging door.

Its architecture was a type of simple classic art,
but in the tragedy of life it played a leading part.
And oft the passing traveler drove slow and heaved a
    sigh
to see the modest hired girl slip out with glances shy.

We had our poesy garden that the women loved so
    well;
I loved it too, but better still I loved the stronger smell
that filled the evening breeze so full of homely cheer
and told the night o'ertaken tramp that human life was
    near.

On lazy August afternoons, it made a little bower,
delightful where my grandsire sat and whiled away an
    hour.
For there the summer morning its very cares entwined,
and berry bushes reddened in the steaming soil behind.

All day fat spiders spun their webs to catch the buzzing
    flies
that flitted to and from the house where Ma was
    baking pies.
And once a swarm of hornets bold, had built a palace
    there,
and stung my unsuspecting aunt—I must not tell you
    where.

Then father took a flaming pole; that was a happy day.
He nearly burned the building up, but the hornets left
    to stay.
When summer's bloom began to fade and winter to
    carouse,
we banked the little building with a heap of hemlock
    boughs.

But when the crust was on the snow and sullen skies
    were grey,
in sooth the building was no place where one could
    wish to stay.
We did our duties promptly; there one purpose swayed
    the mind.
We tarried not, nor lingered long on what we left
    behind.

The torture of that icy seat would make a Spartan sob,
for needs must scrape the goose-flesh with a lacerating cob

that from a frost encrusted nail was suspended by a
string.
My father was a frugal man and wasted not a thing.

When grandpa had to go "out back" and make his
morning call,
we'd bundle off the dear old man with a muffler and a
shawl.
I knew the hole, on which he sat, t'was padded all
around.
And once I dared to sit there, t'was all too wide I
found.

My loins were all too little and I jackknifed there to
stay.
They had to come and get me out, or I'd have passed
away.
Then father said ambition was a thing that boys should
shun,
and I must use the children's hole till childhood days
were done.

But still I marvel at the craft that cut those holes so
true;
the baby hole and the slender hole that fitted sister Sue.
That dear old country landmark; I've tramped around
a bit
and in the lap of luxury my lot has been to sit.

But ere I die, I'll eat the fruit of trees I robbed of yore.
They seek the shanty where my name is carved upon
the door.
I wean the old familiar smell will soothe my faded soul.
I'm now a man, but none the less, I'll try the children's
hole.

(Note: I didn't get a copy of the poem from the man, but he said it was written by James Whitcomb Riley. I tried to find it and had to go through Eva Brubaker who worked in the Nappanee City Library to find a copy. She wrote to the Indiana State Library and received a copy and a note from the state library informing her that the James W. Riley family claims it was not his, so it is without an acknowledged author, but it is funny in my humble opinion.)

Back in the tent trailer days, even in California, we had some unique experiences. One was at Pismo Beach when the family took turns reading the book *Jaws,* sitting on the beach. It was intimidating to swim in the surf after reading that book.

At Lassen National Park in northern California, our son Bruce and I did a cross-country hike, which means no trails, just using the sun and mountains as guides. We had checked at the ranger station for some advice. We had a great time watching deer play in a meadow. At one point we followed them and we lost sight of the tallest mountain so we had to climb a steep mountain to get the right direction. We eventually returned to the tent with Marlene and Bernice.

Bruce and I had a similar experience years later when he was out of high school. We were at Yellowstone National Park. We told Marlene we would be back after a short hike up to a lake. So we drove our pickup truck out to a trailhead. Bernice was now married, so Marlene was alone in our fifth wheel. When we got to the lake, Bruce told me he wanted to hike cross-country back to the campground. I told him he could get lost in the wilderness. I couldn't let him do it alone. He asked, "Well are you going to stand here and argue or go with me?" I told him his mother would be worried, but he insisted so off we went. I also asked how we would get our truck to our campsite. He said he would hike back to get the truck, a couple of miles from our campsite.

We followed animal trails often, kept the western sun to our left since we knew we had to hike north and hopefully we would get to Yellowstone Lake where we were camped on the shoreline. We saw numerous wild animals, were stopped in our tracks by a couple of trumpeter swans that scared us stiff. They make an intense loud racket when they are surprised and take off. We saw a huge elk buck and a well antlered deer. I was glad we didn't see any bear.

The sun was setting and we hadn't seen Yellowstone Lake. I was getting anxious. We finally broke through the woods but we were up on a very high cliff above Yellowstone Lake and some miles from the campground where we could see evening fires and lights twinkling in the distance. There were no easy trails for some time. We had to crawl over logs and go around bushes until we got to flat land where fishermen had made some trails along the lake. It was dark until we got back. Marlene met us with both laughter and tears. A kind neighbor offered to drive us to get our truck. In the morning Marlene baked them a coffee cake. It was early fall so it was quite chilly. These are times we shall always treasure as memories.

One other involvement is my penchant for doing projects. For example when Bruce was in high school he took wood working. I suggested we get a grandfather clock kit and he assisted me in putting that together. It still stands in our home. I must confess I took on a few projects that were beyond me. I enjoyed doing our own home repairs. Once I tried gluing a toaster, but when it wouldn't function, Marlene took it to a local appliance dealer, who also was a member of our local church. He told her to tell me to stick to church work and he would handle appliances. Well, I still love tools and doing projects.

We enjoyed camping and hiking in the Canadian Rockies and had some unique experiences seeing snow avalanches and hearing glaciers creaking as they melted in late summer. We also met a mountain goat on a high mountain trail in a light snow storm. It was awesome. I said of some of these experiences that we worshipped whether we wanted to or not.

Later I enjoyed hiking the Grand Canyon. Across the years I hiked it six times. There were two most memorable hikes. One was all the way from the south rim to the north rim. Marlene and I did this with a group right after she had finished chemotherapy and radiation for breast cancer. She was the first woman out of the canyon in our party. Years later, the last time I hiked the south rim, was with our son, son in law, two grandsons and our youngest granddaughter. That was in December 2003 and Maria was only nine years old. She was the first one out of the canyon. (I discovered later my wife had whispered to Maria, prior to the hike, since she was the only female she should be the first one out of the canyon.)

Our son in law sometimes walked too close to the edge of the trail for my comfort zone and I cautioned him. Bob responded that his feet were so sore he thought falling over the edge was not a bad alternative. He is a comedian but I was slow to catch the humor. I have a fear of heights and so this hike, while a great adventure, at times filled me with terror.

Marlene and I have visited most of the National Parks and we especially enjoy Yosemite and have taken friends and family there when visiting in California. Utah also has more National Parks than most states and they have a variety of beauty. We visited many of these. We enjoyed Death Valley and the story of Scottie's Castle which is an out of the way place to visit, but we thought it was well worth the trip.

Another hobby I enjoy is playing golf. I learned to play when I was a pastor in the late 1950's. On one occasion, J. Harold Engle took me with two friends to play golf. One man was really upset when he made bad shots and would throw his clubs and used profanity frequently. I was thinking he could have profited from a class in anger management. Harold and his friend tried to tell him I was a pastor but he didn't believe them. On the way home, he asked me what my job was and I told him I was Harold's pastor. He paused and then said, "The heck (actually a much stronger word) you are?" He finally believed me and then apologized profusely. I told him it was really his Maker he should consider, not me, since we were strangers. Harold always enjoyed remembering that time.

While living at Nappanee, John Hostetter and Erwin Thomas often played golf with me. When Kevin Ryan was in California he would insist that we play as often as I could get it in. I often resisted, but we had many great times. One day we were playing and we are both very competitive. A stranger had joined us and after he heard us arguing about the number of our strokes, he finally said with a loud voice, "Hey guys, this is just a game!" We were caught off guard and tried to relax, and neither of us left the man know we were ministers.

Also our family physician, James Alderfer, would invite me to play. He was a good golfer and took me on some really nice courses. In later years I have not found a regular partner so golf is less frequent, but it was a great game to focus away from the cares of the church. In recent years Dennis Good and some friends golf when we are able and the weather is decent. Every now and then our son and I play which is always a rewarding time together. Now in Yuma, Arizona, in the winters, I have returned to playing golf.

Living in southern California, we did get to the famed Rose Parade on some occasions. Once we camped with Marlene's brother and wife in their motor home. LG and I agreed to sleep on the sidewalk to save a place to view the parade. He took the first shift and when I went out to relieve him he sent me back to sleep with my wife and said he would stay on the sidewalk. It was a kind move especially since it was a very cold night. The other time we went to the event we had reserved seats in the stands. But over the years we prefer to watch it on television.

I mentioned earlier I had gotten a small motorcycle. I enjoyed riding it and then the larger bikes were also a great relief to ride and escape the routines of life. In our move back to Pennsylvania in 1992 we had sold our Honda Interstate, but found a good used one that was really a nice Honda Aspencade (top of their line at the time). Marlene and I enjoyed some really nice rides including a stint on the Skyline Drive in the state of Virginia.

I had mentioned earlier that I would meet her sister Ernestine and her husband Ira Eyster. They met us for camping and we would occasionally visit in their home in Oklahoma. Ira was a professor at the University of Oklahoma. One advantage they had was tickets to the Oklahoma University football games.

He was considering becoming involved in our church work in the area of stewardship when he died of a heart attack. It was a shock and I believe he would have added much to our church life. They also assisted in a church planting adventure we had initiated in Oklahoma City. Marlene and her sister attended a number of Sooner football games as long as she was able. As she aged and then became very ill in her eighties, Marlene and I made contacts with her sister until her death in 2005.

Chapter 21

Interludes in Drama

Every now and then I would be asked to do something unique. One day, Dorcas Lady Good, a former school mate at Messiah Academy came to my office. She taught drama in the local public school. She asked if I would read a play she had come across and give her my opinion. It was entitled, *Jesus BC 2000.* I told her I would read it.

She returned some time later and I gave her my opinion on the drama. She thanked me and then she asked what she really wanted, "Would you play the part of the Father?" She was actually asking for me to play the part of the Father (God) in the drama and she would direct it at the Upland Brethren in Christ church. I told her some people already thought I was playing the part of God and this would likely get me in some trouble. She did not agree with me and insisted I pray about it and let her know if I would accept her proposal. Since I loved drama back in high school and hadn't done it for a spell, I agreed to accept this diversion.

Actually the drama was well received at the Upland church. Then the following summer Dorcas came back and asked if I would do the drama at General Conference. This was a stretch but I reluctantly agreed knowing there were a few spots in the drama at which some folk would take offense, especially with me playing the role of God the Father! Well I did it and one pastor confronted me saying he would rather have had a man in his pulpit taking God's name in vain than what I had done in the drama. I took him aside in a nearby office and tried to explain the difference between Scripture and drama. There was a painting on the wall of a rocking chair on a porch. In an attempt to explain the subjectivity of art interpretation, I told him I saw an elderly lady in the rocking chair. He looked at me and said, "You have problems!" I don't think I helped him a great deal but he accepted my efforts to assuage his anger. But by far and away the majority of people thought it was a great drama and enjoyed the fact that I was willing to participate.

Dorcas also came to me the third time and asked if I once more would act in the drama, *Jesus BC*. This time she produced and directed the best rendition of the three times she had directed this play. At least she and I shared that opinion. I was by far the oldest member of the cast and was affirmed by the others who played their parts well and we helped each other in case we missed lines. It was fun to do drama once again. Dorcas produced this drama and it ran twice at Riverside Brethren in Christ church on December 22nd and 23rd, 2004.

Once again, at the end of 2005, Dorcas Good called for me to act in a drama, *The Gift of the Magi*. I complied and it took some creative time management to finish the Ontario interim pastorate, which I was doing at the time, and attend play practices. But Dorcas, as usual, had pulled together a talented cast and did a fantastic production. We had three nights of performances, December 21st through 23rd. We had a full house each night at Riverside. Again, I worked with a young cast and it was fun to be the narrator of this wonderful Christmas story drama.

One other drama was a small play I wrote. Marlene and I portrayed this vignette in Abilene, Kansas on the life and times of her grandfather, M. G. Engle.

Chapter 22

Mentors

Along my journey there were persons I came to know and with whom I developed relationships. I believe people impact us and form us. Some of the persons with whom I had strong positive relationships, or even those with whom I had conflict, sharpened me as a person. Most of the people I will mention were or have been friends across the decades. Some of them have already passed from this life to God's Life beyond. Some have chosen to allow differences or distance to diminish our times together but I have respected them and want to mention them here as honored persons in my journey.

During my college days I formed friendships with Harold and Ruth Engle, Joyce and Glenn Ginder, and Charlie and Miriam Byers. It is amazing how we continue to cross each other's pathways after all these years. Now Charlie and Miriam are usually in Indiana or Florida; Harold and Nancy (Harold's first wife, Ruth, died from a rare disease in 2003) live in Pennsylvania. Glenn and Joyce travel the country with their fifth wheel full time serving in a group that helps camps and retreat centers. It is a blessing to have these friendships. E-mail has helped keep us in touch.

During my days as pastor I have already mentioned Henry S. Miller and his wife Sarah. They gave us an affirming initiation into ministry and opened our eyes to see and understand God's people. My bishop during those years was Henry Ginder. He began my lessons on general and regional church life. Far beyond my perception or expectation, I would one day serve with Henry

Ginder as a fellow bishop. The people who served as leaders of the local church at Elizabethtown when I was pastor were helpful advisors. Couples like Paul and Verda Wolgemuth, Walter and Rachel Martin, Martin and Ethel Engle, and John and Anna Kreider come to mind. Ruth Kraybill, an older respected woman, taught me much about "group validators." This was a term I later learned in seminary to refer to people who may not hold office but you better check where they stand on issues since many people will follow them instead of you as the designated leader.

When I became involved in Christian Education, men like Dr. Harold Engle, Dr. Arthur Climenhaga, and Dr. Robert Smith modeled administrative and mature leadership for me. They were superiors I admired and learned from in many ways. I have already written elsewhere about my colleagues, Walter and Lois Wenger and John and Eva Brubaker.

John and Eva became good friends with us in Pennsylvania in the 1960's. John and I had the years together in Congregational Life ministries that were highly treasured. Then our pathways took us to different times and places. Both of us had retired from full time active ministry by 2008. We try to meet at least every two months, along with Dennis and Dorcas Good. All six of us now reside in California. John and Eva and Dennis and Dorcas are esteemed friends.

I have decided to include persons involved with me during the years I was Bishop and General Secretary in an appendix since many readers will not know them.

Appendix A (These are additional people I worked with during 1972-1984.)

Chapter 23

Mentoring

Since I had been so blest by my parents, grandparents, Pastor Sam Wolgemuth, and my spiritual father, Henry S. Miller, I wanted to share my life with others. I discovered over the years that many times it was part of my life, especially the years when I was bishop. But I was surprised years later to hear that some younger men looked to me as their mentor and I was not even aware I was mentoring them.

In my early days of ministry I always appreciated younger people who came to me as pastor. One young man was Frank Moquin. He came from a family outside the church. He had a very inquisitive mind and we spent many hours discussing theology and philosophy. He eventually married Sue Martin, one of the young women of the congregation. I can only hope my investment of time and energy helped him along the way.

There were a number of youth in the church and school mates that I related to over the years. I remember Harold, Richard, and Jerry Engle, three sons of Martin and Ethel Engle, a strong family in the Elizabethtown church. I treasured the many times we had with these men, their family and their friends. Paul Wolgemuth, Jr. was a young man who became the first "Herald of Christ" youth in an organization that would be similar to an "eagle scout." The Paul and Verda Wolgemuth family were special deacons to us in our pastoral days.

I mentioned earlier that when I invited Kevin and Gail Ryan to become pastor of Zion, Kansas, we formed a special friendship. I spent many hours with my friend Kevin. We spent hours on golf courses enjoying nature, but especially checking on each other's count of strokes on the course. We would share books, argue, debate, reason and disagree, but our love and friendship has been strong even though in the last decades of my life I reside in California and he in Pennsylvania. We have kept in touch by e-mail and occasional visits when possible.

One younger man whom I met during his seminary days was Ken Letner. Our paths crossed frequently and he later followed my trail in Christian Education. But it was not until he was a pastor that I was surprised to read his story in his bishop's newsletter and note that he considered me as one of his most respected mentors. In my senior years in 2002 Ken was instrumental in having me come and be an interim pastor for the church he had pastored, Cedar Grove near Mifflintown, Pennsylvania. He had become bishop of that region. I stayed with him and his wife Linda and their son James still at home. I realized how much this relationship had meant to me. It was a shock in 2008 when we learned Ken had brain cancer and died an untimely death in September of 2008. His story is part of my times.

Another young man, Perry Engle (who happens to be my wife's nephew) grew up in southern California. During the years I was still living in California, we would meet monthly to dialogue and prayerfully share each other's journey. He was planting a new church and so we had a lot in common. It was a serendipity when, years later, he became a bishop in southern California. Then, in my senior years, he employed me for a couple of years as a consultant to two church planters. It has been a mutually enriching relationship with Perry and Marta and their three lovely daughters.

Not many readers will know all the pastors and spouses I worked with but I have memories of special times in the face of challenges, crises, health or career times or just plain living life together with the couples.

I want to include the names of the relationships that were rewarding to me and hopefully to the pastors and spouses that we met on our journey. By the way, some of my favorite sayings, certainly not original with me, but which I would often repeat were:

"Life is a journey not a destination." Or another way I said it was, "The process is the goal." Or I would say, "Whatever you think of yourself is less than what God thinks of you." At some of the pastors and spouses retreats I would hear my often-used statements quoted back to me. At least I knew I was communicating something of my philosophy of life.

I believe strongly that every pastor and spouse with whom I worked had great value. It would be interesting to include remarks about each couple but that moves beyond my biography. So I have listed them in an appendix.

(See **pastors and spouses** in alphabetical order in **Appendix B**.)

For those who read through these names it may be a bit like the genealogies of the Old Testament, but in reality they are people who enriched and formed me as a person. I thank God for each and every one. The boy who became a bishop was blest with many people who made my ministry meaningful. With these people I laughed, loved, and lifted.

I have included in the next chapter notes that pastors and spouses wrote about me.

Chapter 24

Pastors and Spouses Wrote

In 1984 when I had completed twelve years of being a bishop, a scrapbook was put together for us and presented at my farewell.

Below are some quotes from pastors and wives who were then serving in the Pacific Conference. It speaks for them and I regret I don't have similar notes from the pastors and spouses that served in the Midwest Conference. But we have memories from those couples just as valuable as the notes below.

> "We want to thank you for being a model couple—'a couple of nuts'—who have linked their lives together for our benefit. Thanks for your model of openness and realness in the ministry."
>
> Ed and Pat Ashby

> "With heartfelt gratitude we thank you for the many times you have represented grace to us. Thank you for the beauty of your lives in which we continue to perceive many principles which speak to our souls in voiceless and invisible ways."
>
> Herb and Ruth Anderson

"You two have so much to give to other couples. You have often spoken the very words we needed to encourage and strengthen us. We thank the Lord for both of you and want you to know how much we appreciate and love you."

Jim and Lillian Bailey

"You are Thanksgiving, Christmas and Easter all wrapped up in one happy couple.—Thanksgiving, because you are so grateful and affirming of your pastors.—Christmas, because you are so giving of yourselves to others.—Easter, because you are so vibrant with life and encouraging to us."

Amos and Alice Buckwalter

"A good bishop is rather to be chosen than great riches. Your caring for the person, the feelings, and the dignity of people over the position, the office, the situation, has been an inspiration and an affirmation of the example of Christ. You and Marlene without pretension have brought an appealing dimension to the office of bishop."

Bob and Mary Lou Bushnell

"Your acceptance of us as we were is what gave us the courage to 'go for it.' At a time in our lives when God wanted us to minister to others, you opened the door wide for us and helped us on the journey of serving God and his people."

Fred and Caroline Carter

"We thank you for the wonderful privilege of having you all as our personal friends, brother and sister, and our spiritual leaders during the past ten plus years of our ministry together. Never to be forgotten are the times when your words of confidence, affirmation, or instruction have put us back together, as it were, and on our way doing the work God has called us to do."

LeRoy and Judy Eberly

"You and Marlene were ready to put yourselves on the line as you formed the Double Triumvirate that sent the church planting idea into orbit. Both of you have been able to relate to reality and at the same time maintain your vision."

Gordon and Eunice Engle

"Don you have the talent to make people feel special. We also appreciate your honesty, humor, and balanced walk with our Lord. Marlene, when we think of you we'll always be reminded of blackberries!"

Jim and Terry Ernst
(Marlene loved to make pies with Oregon blackberries when we visited the Redwood Country church in Grants Pass, Oregon.)

"Our friendship has been generously and equally filled with tears of joys and tears of sorrow. We talked about our hurts, our fears, as he patiently and compassionately listened. Somehow in the midst of our brokenness, his caring brought worth and meaning to us as individuals and as a couple. Love is healing."

Jack and Jeanine Finley

"Thank you for reaching out to include us and involve us with other couples in ministry. Thank you for your warmth, your laughter, and your honesty,"

Bruce and Sandy Finfrock

"You have given to us in the eleven years we have worked together something of the making of a 'pastor's heart.' You have touched our family. In that touch has been the making of priorities that feed and nourish relationships."

Sam and Mary Fisher

"You have helped us to make our move to the Brethren in Christ a very positive decision. We have appreciated so much your affirmation, encouragement, evaluation, and also your loving confrontation. We have relied on your wise counsel, and many times and it has been very helpful to us as a family. Thank you for caring."

Ron and Marilyn Freeman

"To two very special people, whose friendship has been closer to us than any other friendship over a span of thirty plus years, whose leadership has modeled compassion, expertise, honesty and brotherhood, who have functioned primarily as brother and sister whether in the role of bishop, fellow pastor or friend."

Glenn and Joyce Ginder

"To write to you is to share with dear friends. Thank you for expressing to us in so many ways this special quality of Christian love and supportive friendship. Thank you for: the risk of faith, the spirit of availability, and supportive listening. Finally, in being yourselves, warmly human, yet sensibly spiritual, and best of all our friends."

Bob and Barbara Hempy

"Marlene, you are such a neat lady. You balance out Don perfectly. If it hadn't been for your advice Bishop Don, plus of course God's guidance and love, we would have left our great opportunity for ministry."

Kevin and Candy Longenecker

"A man of faith, hope and love. As I became friends and a fellow worker with you, I realized that these were the attributes that constitute your life. These also are the gifts you gave to all. Thank you, Don and Marlene, for your faith, for your joy, for your hope, for your love, and for your prayers, without which I would not attain what the Lord has for me."

Cal and Pat Morey

"You have been a tremendous influence and leadership model to our lives and to the Living Word ministry. It was your vision, your willingness, and your concern that has made our fellowship a living reality. Many souls will unknowingly owe gratitude to you forever."

Freddy and Pat Negrete

"We want to let you know that we have been blessed by having you as Bishop. We felt that we always knew exactly where we stood in relationship with you which has made it comfortable to be working with you and has allowed us to be honest with you."

John and Kathleen Neufeld

"We thank you for always being there when the family needed you, in cloudy times and brighter days also. We remember your listening ear and your hearing heart. You are reachable and touchable."

Floyd and Beth Speck

"It has been fun to dream and plan together about church growth for our conference. We appreciate your vision for evangelism and for the increase of our conference church membership enrollment. We will always be happy about our share in helping those things happen. We appreciate your keen insights and genuine spirituality."

Aaron and Martha Stern

"Your lives and testimony have been a genuine inspiration and encouragement to us. You have ministered to us and we and our people have always been inspired and challenged through your presentation of God's Word."

Keith and Edith Whitford

For my farewell as Bishop in the Pacific Conference they planned an evening of reminiscing at the Upland Brethren in Christ Church. Ron Freeman was in charge and he had his three daughters who were now teenagers on the platform. He related the story of me playing games with the girls and how the one crept into the bedroom and crawled into bed with me on my first visit in their home, when she was only three. She was seated on the floor and raised a sign that read, "The Lucky One." The tables were turned and now I was blushing and embarrassed. In the Midwest they also honored me and presented me with a western hat and cowboy boots. I loved the people and churches of both conferences. My life was incredibly enriched during the years I served as Bishop.

Chapter 25

Grandchildren

The stories of the births, activities, and adventures of our four grandchildren enriched and blest my life.

The first was our grandson, Bryce Robert, son of our daughter, Bernice, and our son in law, Bob. They waited nine years before having any children. On a number of our visits with them I would ask if I forgot to explain something. Bernice would say, "Oh, Dad!" We were eager to become grandparents.

Bryce was born over the weekend of Easter, March 24th, 1989. Our daughter and I had mutual thoughts about the pain of delivery and the joy of the new grandson that coincided with Good Friday and Easter Sunday Day of Resurrection. Bob and Marlene were in the delivery area. Bob's mom, Norma, and I were the anxious grandparents in the waiting room. We are both talkers, but as the hours passed we ran out of words. We were anxious to hear reports and finally we were invited to the area to see the new grandson among the new infants. He was a large baby and not hard to identify. He weighed in at 10 pounds and 11 ounces. So of course it was a hard birth. He was a healthy boy and is now a tall young man at least 6'7" tall. We, of course, spoiled him as much as we could. Bryce was always eager to explore. By his first Christmas he was ready to pull ornaments from the Christmas tree. He was always into numerous sports.

Bryce was always a risk taker. He would spend a lot of time on a skateboard and wanted us to watch him *take air* as he put it. In short he would get a run, jump off a ramp into the air and try spinning and landing on the board. He has been an avid bike rider since youth and several times had to call his parents about accidents. Some were scary, but he evaded serious injuries and kept us and his parents on the edge of anxiety.

As a doting grandfather, I allowed Bryce to try driving before he was licensed. He sat so tall no one really questioned him driving. Of course when he gained a driver's license his penchant for risk was still there and he had a couple of accidents and, like most young men, learned the hard way about cars and traffic hazards. Bryce was always a joy on camping outings. He was a good hiker of the Grand Canyon.

With his height advantage he excelled in basketball and volleyball in his high school days. We often went to his games. After his high school graduation he decided on a year in photographic studies at the Art Institute of Chicago. One of his photographs hangs in our hallway at our home.

In 2010-2011 Bryce was on a rowing team at the University of California, San Diego. In 2011-12, he went to Hong Kong to visit and to study. His girlfriend's parents come from that part of the world. So Bryce has introduced us to a possibility of being an international family.

Our second grandchild was also born to our daughter and husband. She was named Leesann Noelle, and arrived just before Christmas on December 20, 1990. It was obvious to observe right from the beginning that she was a beautiful redhead. Once again Norma and I awaited the news of the birth. This time we did not have long to wait and we were invited to be with our daughter and the newborn baby girl.

She is quite creative and has provided us with numerous childhood stories. When she was only two she once escaped the backyard, wearing nothing but her birthday suit, and her dad chased her around the block. Leesann loves dancing and as a little girl I took her to dancing class. I was watching from a point unknown to her and she was clearly a non-conformist. She danced her own way. Upon arriving home, her dad asked, "Think she will be a Rockette?" We both laughed, knowing she would not likely fit into a pattern like the rest.

Leesann always loved beauty and once she found a letter on a neighbor's mail box, outgoing mail, with a beautiful stamp. She took it home. As her mother told the story, I queried whether Leesann would always tell the truth. Her mom said, "Dad she came out lying!" I didn't want to hear it but we all know we are born with the capacity to shade the truth. Leesann finally confessed and the letter, which contained a check, was restored to the neighbor.

Leesann loved camping with her cousin Maria and they were both lovers of the swimming pool. We were proud attendees at sports events when she was a cheerleader in high school. She almost became a part of the queen's court for the famed Rose Parade in Pasadena, California. She was in the last seventy-five candidates out of over a thousand. She is now a student at the University of California, Santa Cruz. We are biased of course but she is a striking beautiful young woman. She is most thoughtful and sends affirming notes as a loving granddaughter. In the spring of 2011 Marlene and I visited her in Santa Cruz along with my sister Thelma and her husband Bill. In the summer of 2012 we learned she will be spending time this next school year in Ireland, so the saga continues.

Our third grandchild, Dylan Horst, was born to our son, Bruce and Carol. He arrived on August 7th, 1991. At the time we were in Colorado at an Engle family reunion. When we received the call we left immediately and headed west to be with this young lad who would bear the Shafer family name. As a boy he loved me pushing him on a swing as high as I could. He also was part of a tree house project that his dad and I built in a large oak tree on their property. As a boy he enjoyed building things such as Lego projects and made creations of his own.

He had a skateboard with larger wheels and built his own track on a rather steep hill at his home. We enjoyed his antics and daring rides. We enjoyed watching him play soccer.

Dylan started young and became an accomplished classical guitar player and was repeatedly invited to play at the local Tehachapi community chorus events as a featured guest. He played at local restaurants and was rewarded with donations in his open guitar case.

As an artist he did a pencil art rendition of Marlene and me and it hangs in our hallway at home. As with his cousin, I also allowed him to drive before he was licensed. It was in a private park and some perfectionist spotted Dylan and asked if he had a license. I simply told him to stop and I took the driver's seat. I explained to him some folks have *anal retention* and explained the term. He enjoyed the laughter and forgot the embarrassment I caused him.

Dylan was one of the two highest academic students at the head of his high school class and gave an excellent salutatorian speech. He hiked the Grand Canyon with his cousin Bryce.

Dylan liked to arm wrestle with me and his dad. Of course we are no longer a match. His torso is very muscular since he has been on a rowing team at the University of California Los Angeles. Indeed he is the captain of his team and recently was featured in an advertisement about the 2012 summer Olympics.

Our fourth and last grandchild, Maria Katherine, is another beautiful young lady. She was born on May 15th, 1994. She has been a violin player and won a place in the California old time fiddler's contest as an eight year old. Bruce looked at me and said, "Well dad, we know those genes didn't come from our side of the family." Maria plays violin in the local community orchestra. In addition she played a saxophone and was in the local high school band.

She loves to play table games with the family. She was the youngest hiker on the Grand Canyon adventure. Maria was also a competitive basketball and soccer player. She has also excelled as a cross-country runner.

She has been a thoughtful young lady and sends us e-mails often. Maria and her cousin, Leesann, often put words and artwork on our white board in the hallway at our home when they visit. Maria also placed in a young teen talent contest. She graduated as a senior in the class of 2012, which we attended at the Tehachapi High School. She was third in her class and received numerous honors.

All four are involved in the University of California, Bryce at San Diego, Leesann at Santa Cruz, Dylan and his sister Maria are both at UCLA in the fall of 2012.

As you might guess, we are pleased with and proud of our four grandchildren. During the years they were children or young teens we took them camping, usually two at a time, the girls and then the boys. We would plan to have the families together as often as we could arrange it. And even in spite of my schedule, we arranged to be at events in which they were involved letting them know we appreciated their talents and skills. Now they are all young adults and continue to bless our journey of life.

Daughter's family, Bernice, Leesann, Bryce, and Bob

Son's family, Carol, Maria, Dylan and Bruce

Grandchildren with us, 2006

Chapter 26

General Secretary

The process of leaving the role of bishop had some interesting dynamics. At that time there was a limit of twelve years to serve as bishop. I personally led the move to base service on evaluation and not tenure. So years later (1994), there would be no limit on the number of years a bishop could serve. The tenure on general church administrators was removed the year I left denominational work in 1996.

I was asked to serve on the search committee for the General Secretary in 1984 as I completed twelve years as a regional bishop. If I recall correctly, there were nine or ten members in the search group and most of us were eligible and willing to be a nominee. It made the process interesting. But the most intense dynamic for me personally was a phone call from Arthur Climenhaga, who was finishing his term as General Secretary.

He indicated he would only fill out the closing time of his term if I would be the nominee and he would inform the search committee of his decision. I told him one possibility would be that the search committee might sense they were being pressured and perhaps we might both be out. Knowing there were a number of interested candidates, I wondered if this challenge might take him out in finishing his term and me out as a nominee. He said it was a risk he would take if I would allow my name to go forward. As it turned out, I was eventually asked to serve.

The administrative work took me away from many of my close relational ties. It is my self-perception, and others have also affirmed, that relationships are my strength. But I gave my best to help the denomination think about the future. I attempted to help them set goals and work at reducing personnel and expenditures at the denominational level. As I reflect back, I saw my work as having at least several dimensions. It was leadership, administration, communication, education, and motivation. Thus, I worked on church order, church relations, evaluation, ministries of teaching and preaching. We also worked on core values and attempted to motivate our churches to keep growth as a central issue.

If I were to summarize these years, it was to focus the church on less general church boards, less meetings, less expense on gatherings that seemed to me did not produce change nor result in any obvious progress. I had been mentored to keep church leadership as a team in contrast to a business model with one executive at the top.

Henry Miller had told me the church is not a business, but we could learn from business how to do the work of the church. The church is a voluntary community following Jesus Christ. He warned that some gifted people can lead a movement, but if total trust and authority is put in one person, power can corrupt. Even the most gifted and spiritual person should not carry that burden alone. Brother Miller insisted Jesus should remain the sole leader of the church. It sure made sense to me. Therefore I insisted on a team of leaders. For a while we had four leaders, but eventually there was pressure to reduce that to two. Also some businessmen offered to provide resources to build a church office building, which gave the denomination a physical headquarters.

Since I was living in California in 1984, I was reluctant to move to Pennsylvania, which some leaders wanted me to do. Since the denomination had not required its officers to move to Pennsylvania in previous years, they allowed me to stay in California. But in 1992 when the denominational office was built, the General Conference Board requested the general church leaders to move to Pennsylvania.

We each and all agreed to that move. In many ways it facilitated better teamwork between the administrators in North

America and overseas ministries. The offices included church administrators, financial and stewardship leaders, and world mission executives who were brought together. Accountability was enhanced, community was improved, but old patterns are hard to break and it took some deliberate work to change the old ways of independent operations.

During these years (1984-1992) I traveled the country and the world as noted in previous sections. One of the unique things before we had a church headquarters in a building was the quarterly meeting of church leaders. These were often held in homes of the bishops or general church leaders. They were times of review, counsel and setting a vision and plans for the future.

It is hard to tell many stories of board and committee meetings. But those sessions kept the leaders as a team and fostered good communication and accountability.

During the years I was still in Upland as General Secretary (1984-1992), I traveled frequently to the east. It was a condition that I agreed to if I wanted to stay in the west. I didn't mind because our denomination has always had what I would call an "eastern cultural bent." And frankly, I liked the west and our family had settled in California. What I perceived was that even the people who moved west in the early 1900's still had some of the eastern cultural mind-set.

I grew up in the east, but as a lad and young man I was mentored by a pastor with a global vision. Sam Wolgemuth, when leaving the pastorate in Pennsylvania, went with Youth for Christ International and also served on our World Mission Board for a number of years. He instilled in me a vision much larger than I would experience in Lancaster County, Pennsylvania. So I decided to stay as long as possible in California to help the denomination remember it was much more than an eastern, especially Pennsylvanian, denomination.

Consequently, I was frequently debating with brothers and sisters of our churches who wanted to be sure to keep our historical roots and practices. By the time I became a bishop in the early 1970's we had moved beyond the legalisms of dress codes and certain practices. It was summed up in a quip that used to circulate among conservative churches. "Don't play cards, smoke or chew and especially don't date girls who do."

Like most people in America our traditional people in the eastern part of the United States and Canada had moved off farms and into suburbia. We were fast becoming acculturated. Of course some of our people who were more traditional and part of the church families saw this as a threat. But other new people and youth moving to the cities and suburbia saw it as liberating. I saw the changes as a challenge to give some guidance on focusing the denomination on outreach without losing the key values of our heritage.

Don speaking at General Conference, 1985

I gave many hours to dialogue on those issues. I led numerous seminars on evangelism and church growth. I also worked with my colleagues to build community, keep the faith of our fathers and, at the same time, reach out to a changing society and world. I found the twelve years in the role as General Secretary challenging and fulfilling.

For at least twelve years I served with the Mennonite Central Committee on the United States Board and also on the Bi-National Board that included Canada. But we focused on the whole world's needs. It was a major cross-cultural experience as well as a learning experience of how a non-government agency could help people suffering and in need in many countries of the world.

Don at Mennonite Central Committee

We moved to Pennsylvania in the summer of 1992, an interesting time for Marlene and me. It was difficult to leave our biological family in California, but moving back near the campus of Messiah College was meaningful since that is where we met and started our journey together as a married couple.

We were not sure where we would live, but through the help of a realtor, we located a house in a beautiful wooded area called White Rock Acres. It had Boiling Springs, Pennsylvania, as our address, but we were several miles away from that little village. Coming from Messiah College we drove back a winding road that followed the Yellow Breeches Creek, and then turned up a hill into a dense wooded area covered with tall oak and pine trees. We lived almost at the top of this range of the Allegheny Mountains. I often experienced a sense of worship as I drove the route between our home and the church office. The Appalachian

Trail ran right through this section. We never did find out how a developer got such prime land, since most areas like this in Pennsylvania are preserved as state or federal land.

We loved our house that had a Cape Cod type architecture. It had two stories with dormer windows in the roof that were part of the upstairs. It had a wood stove in a family room that separated the house from the garage. We spent many hours there especially on winter evenings. A small herd of deer and numerous families of bushy tailed squirrels and multiple species of birds, especially the large pileated wood pecker, entertained us out of our rear windows. The only down side was the deer eating flowers and the squirrels stealing our bird feed. We loved the setting and the house.

While we were there, we had a garage built by an Amish man and his helpers. It matched the architecture of our house. It sheltered our fifth wheel camper and gave us extra storage. We had a driveway which was rather long and we had it paved after I tried blowing snow and too many stones would be blown on the lawn or into the woods.

House in Boiling Springs, PA 1992-2000

It was hard to leave our children and grandchildren when we moved to Pennsylvania. I recall many times when I would travel from Pennsylvania to California and always find time to spend with them. When it came time to leave and return east I would control my emotions in front of the grandchildren but driving away from either of their homes I would have tears well up in my eyes. It gave me a painful ache to leave them. During the eight years we were east (1992-2000), we always kept in contact with the family by way of letters, phone calls and scheduled visits. When I was west, it was a joy to visit them. Marlene didn't get west as often as I, so she planned times to have them come east or we would go west as often as we could arrange it or afford it. This was the hardest part of moving east.

Beyond our physical location, we had to decide where to tie into a congregation. We were invited to several churches and the choices are plentiful for our denomination in that area. We finally settled on the Grantham Brethren in Christ church, which at the time was located in the heart of the Messiah College Campus and served as the Campus Church.

One of the factors in our decision was when Pastor Bob Ives, sensing Marlene's love of sports, hosted us to a college soccer game. Now that impressed Marlene and I also knew being in a larger church had some advantages when we would need to miss a number of Sundays due to the nature of my work.

We also enjoyed Pastor Ives's preaching and a Sunday school class. It was in one session of a Sunday school class that we met and made friends with Dale and Marian Bomberger. We had never met them prior to being in this Sunday school class together. One Sunday Dale was teaching and he mentioned how many people were being downsized in their jobs. He mentioned in passing, as a social worker for the state, he really did not want recycled ministers coming to be social workers. Dale had a unique sense of humor and I gathered that he liked poking fun at the clergy and the short sides of church life. After he made several more comments about ministers, I raised my hand and told Dale that as a church leader we liked to recycle social workers into ministry in case he ever got a pink slip. His response was "Well, brother, in this case it would take a miracle!" I couldn't help myself so I replied, "Well, Dale, that is the heart of the church's business." The class responded in hearty laughter and Dale blushed. I went to him after class and apologized for being disrespectful. He waved my apology off and said "Anyone that can cut me off at the knees like that has to make a good friend."

And that was the beginning of us learning to know each other. We ended up in a Bible study with Dale and Marian. Then we both purchased dine-out coupons and would eat out together about once a month. We always enjoyed each other's company and laughter seemed to bring us close. We shared with each other our mutual life stories that included both high points and valleys as well. A trust and bond formed that ties us together until the present. Even after we moved back to California, Dale and Marian (who live in Dillsburg, Pennsylvania) keep in mutual contact via e-mail and visits.

Another great joy was having our two children and their families come to visit us in White Rock Acres. The grandchildren seemed to love the place and especially when they came in the winter. Our daughter Bernice and her family especially loved snow which they had not experienced much except in the mountains in California. Bruce's family lived at a higher elevation so they would experience light snow in California.

My mother made a memorable visit to our home in the winter of 1998. She came to see me since I had fallen on a golf course while on a trip to California and tore a ligament in my knee. While visiting me, she suddenly fell asleep or so we thought. My sister, Doris, who brought her, is a nurse and quickly sensed Mother was not breathing and told me to call 911. I did and in less than ten minutes paramedics swarmed our place.

By the time they arrived my mother had revived from whatever happened. But she was taken by ambulance to the Carlisle hospital and then transferred to a hospital in Gettysburg where she lived. My wife had accompanied my sister and mother to the hospitals.

When Marlene came home she said my mother was doing well and appeared to be on the mend. But about 4:00 a.m. the next morning, we received a phone call that my mother had a heart attack and did not survive. It was the end of a good life. Mother was 86 and had been a strong wife, good mother and spiritual presence in our home and family life. I was honored to share some remarks at her memorial service even though I was on crutches.

A Cauldron of Conflict

During the years in administration, we would often deal with issues of disagreement and find our way to some unity. There was one episode and it went on for years. Those involved will recall names and have different views. There are reams of papers, files and letters in the denominational archives that may someday be studied with interest. I share some of that messy affair because it has plagued every denomination and is a heated issue. It had to do with accusations of homosexuality or bisexuality, a very complicated and controversial issue.

In brief, one of our respected lay leaders was accused of inappropriate behavior with some young men in counseling. The general church carried responsibility since the man, although never a credentialed minister, was an officer on one of our general church boards. As far as we could determine, none of the young men involved were minors. I was personally sent to confront the man and I should have remembered the wise words of Scripture to have such matters witnessed by two or three. As it turned out, he denied any wrongdoing. I told him what he shared with me as part of his practice was crossing boundaries and the church leaders deemed it inappropriate. We had him meet with two professionals in the field of psychology and psychiatry. He was counseled, mentored and held accountable by a local church group. But no matter how hard we tried there were some folk dissatisfied with our attempts to correct matters. There were even some potential legal threats. But after more meetings and communications than anyone would want to read about, it was eventually put to rest.

Some church leaders met with one young man involved and his family in which we tried to clarify issues and communication. It was for most a redemptive meeting. While all were agreed that some of the conflict would likely always be a part of our memories, we discerned that we had to let it go. The man accused eventually left the local church and the denomination.

It was a sad chapter in the time of my leadership. We sought the help of pastors, lay leaders and professionals to help us discern our way through this caldron of conflict. But honestly, knowing all the persons involved, I don't know how we could have been more open and willing to listen to help all involved. I am sure some would disagree but such was part of being a leader.

Winds of Change in Career

As we neared the end of my twelve years as General Secretary, a few things happened that led me to decide on a career change. When I had been asked to move to Pennsylvania, I talked with Harvey Sider who had taken the role of Moderator. He told me straight out that he would not continue to live in Pennsylvania beyond 1996. So, when we decided to move to Pennsylvania, it seemed clear that Harvey would return to Canada in four years. That would open the way for me to finish my career up to a normal retirement age. Harvey and other church leaders communicated this sense of the future and encouraged us to make this move.

So Harvey became Moderator and I was General Secretary. We served along with John Byers as Director of Bishops and Harold Chubb as Treasurer. My colleague, Harvey Sider, made a major choice in 1995 that would bring a dramatic turn in the road for me.

One of the changes that came in the structure of the church was the move to two church leaders instead of four. I was not pleased with this decision or trend since it seemed to move more toward a hierarchy form of governance instead of a Biblical model of team leadership.

Early in 1996 I informed Harvey that I would not be available to serve beyond the summer of 1996 since there was still a tenure limitation on the role of General Secretary. He disagreed since he was sure the tenure limitation would be removed, but I had already decided to change my course of action. I decided it was a time for change for me. I did assure him I would give my all to remove the tenure issue since it had failed at the previous General Conference. I felt that at the 1994 Conference I did not have the support of my colleagues when the issue came to a vote. But in 1996 it was removed.

As I reflect back, I was becoming increasingly uncomfortable with the general church boards being involved in focusing on management by objectives more than leaders operating as a team. There was especially the influence and power of some strong lay leaders directing us to be more focused as a business model rather than being a church. It seemed to me there was more movement toward being a corporate model of leading by management than being a church of voluntary people led by leaders.

We spent a fair amount of time, energy and money on centralizing our "church headquarters" symbolized by the building on the campus of Messiah College. This was a trend on implementing "business and management" principles into the ordering of church life. There was a major shift of fewer clergy on our general church boards and populating them with business people and educators. In my perception, it had a profound impact on the "soul of the Brethren in Christ." It is not my intent to make judgment statements, but rather an observation of a major shift in focus and energy.

We were struggling with the national drift from general church to regionalism and more local church autonomy. A lot of focus was shifting as the "older" leadership was leaving. I have reflected that, in some ways, I was a "bridge" between those leaders and the "younger" leaders we have installed since 2000. For example, a major shift in choosing leaders took place during this period. Earlier the Brethren would prayerfully and deliberately choose leaders they deemed gifted and equipped through a process of nominating and having regional and general people lay hands on these selected and approved leaders. From 1996 on it seemed to me we were moving in a new direction. In more recent years, likely after 2000, persons were applying for jobs or were invited to fill out applications to take significant leadership roles. (This could be documented in noting the change from "nominating" groups to "search committees" and "appointments".)

So in light of all these developments and having spent close to four decades in a church vocation, I was looking for a turn in my career path and I came to an open door.

I have tried to respect and support all those who have followed me in leadership. I have been open to share anything but have refrained from making any judgments. It seems to me each generation must discern their ways to lead the church.

Chapter 27

Public Relations

I decided after serving the church in various roles for nearly forty years, I was ready for a change. After prayerful discernment, counsel with my wife, and several other trusted friends, I opened myself to other options. So when I was invited to serve at Messiah Village (changed to Lifeways in 2012) as Director of Public Relations, it was a radical change. It was a good time in many ways. Emerson Lesher, president of Messiah Village, who employed me, had been a lad in elementary school when I was in college. So I knew him and, sitting in his office, I had a sense that life was moving on. It was an eye opener to work on a campus that was composed of seniors. Some lived independently in cottages or apartments. Others had moved into assisted living quarters and, of course, there were those in special care and those who needed medical assistance just short of hospital or hospice care. The Village had a creative section for those suffering with Alzheimer's disease.

One of the serendipities was meeting new people. I worked in the Messiah Village office with Louise Pantzner and Vicky Miculita who came from Roman Catholic and Episcopalian backgrounds. It was refreshing to work with two people who had experience and knowledge of working in our church's fairly large retirement community. For a short time I also worked with Charles Few who had a United Church of Christ background. So it was an ecumenical experience with my fellow employees.

I also joined the local Camp Hill Chamber of Commerce and got involved in the Harrisburg community. It was exciting to learn to meet new people and associate in business circles as contrasted to church circles. President Lesher had given me numerous affirmations and notes in writing that I was doing a great job. I worked on advertising, building displays and keeping our churches aware of the services of Messiah Village.

I also had the pleasure of relating with some of my former teachers and colleagues who were now residents of the Village. Henry Ginder, Charlie Byers, Arthur Climenhaga, K. B Hoover, Isaiah Harley, Paul Hostetler and Paul McBeth were some of the many I knew. Some of my parishioners from Elizabethtown were also residents. Among those were Paul and Verda Wolgemuth, Rachel Martin and Lillian Flowers. It was always a joy to greet them on campus.

One of my assignments was to work with a group called "The Singing Men." I went to their practices frequently. When they went on the road to sing for churches, I would accompany them and promote Messiah Village. They were a good public relations contact for the Village.

One of the events that almost happened was getting Messiah Village an appearance on national television. *Good Morning America* had sent a team to interview our residents and administrators. We were to have a spot on the news, but we received word that we had been bumped by Diane Sawyer who had some friends she wanted on that specific morning. But it had been fun to see our people interact with the news media. One lady who was over 100 years old was on the computer. When she was asked how she learned, she replied, pointing to her head, "Well the chips are a little slower but they still work."

After four years I was informed I no longer had a job. It was a very difficult time for me. My wife, who is always supportive of me, helped me move on during these tough times. She indicated the dismissal got us back to California just a little earlier than anticipated. It was a move we wanted to eventually make to be closer to our children and grandchildren in our senior years.

There were some really nice factors during my four years at Messiah Village. My sister in law, Sharon Engle, wife of Marlene's younger brother, was employed as a Director of Development in the same office area as I was employed. She replaced Charles Few who had been "downsized" ahead of me. It brought us closer as family and friends.

At Christmas time, Marlene and I often hosted the public relations and development office staff from Messiah Village in our home. We had gift exchanges that were a lot of fun and we will always have pleasant memories of those occasions.

I also had the privilege of performing the marriage ceremony for my assistant Louise Pantzner and Clint Smith. We worked together well and we gave Messiah Village the logo they still use to this day, "Enhancing Life." I also found a friend in Vicky Miculita that has continued. Marlene and I still connect with Vicky and her husband, Gary, when we have the opportunity. She was also let go from the Village several years after I left.

So it was a joy to find new friends and connect with some family and old friends. The experience of being "downsized" also gave me a new understanding for people I would meet over the next several years as I returned to parish ministry. I had a new empathy for people who give years of service and suddenly are told they no longer have a job and are now facing an unknown future. It includes feelings of anger and insecurity that I would not have understood had I not experienced the pain of being left go at Messiah Village.

Marlene was still employed at Messiah College and her positive attitude gave me encouragement. I did experience the support of our family. Our son Bruce sent me a note he had titled, **"Just a Word of Encouragement."** He wrote, "*I have always been proud of your achievements throughout your career. The way you have been an agent for change, the way people respond to you, and your willingness to be vulnerable are a few of the things that come to mind as I look back. As you go forward don't sell yourself short. I believe those who know you have more respect and appreciation for your skills than you might think. Things tend to work out for the best. PLUS, look at what else you have in this life: friends, family (good looking and above average), a great spouse (sitting on a bucket* *of money), health (everything still works), a house with trees and deer and birds (too bad for the squirrels), etc."* It was an encouraging word.

Both of our children and their spouses have been very affirming. As adults they return much of the respect and love Marlene instilled in our children. Marlene's kindness toward our children's spouses has also blest us.

Bernice and Bruce, with their families, have always blest our marriage and the older we grow the more we appreciate their love and support. So, Marlene and I turned our lives together toward another phase and eventually headed back to California just a bit earlier than we had anticipated.

Chapter 28

Medical Detours

In the spring of 1981, I had been to Pennsylvania and spoke sixteen times including a series of Lenten services at the Carlisle Brethren in Christ Church, taught some classes at Messiah College and led a few seminars. I developed hoarseness in my voice. I thought it was a sore throat. But after numerous trips to our family doctor and a specialist, I was told to be silent for a week. For those who know me, this was virtually impossible. When I returned to the throat specialist, he insisted I be quiet for another week. This time I never uttered a word. It really was possible! I wrote a lot of notes.

Finally on August 13, 1981, following a biopsy, we were informed of the diagnosis of cancer of the larynx. We had the choice of surgery, which would have meant I would no longer speak normally but through a device in my neck, or to take our chances with radiation.

It was easy to decide since my whole career involved the use of my voice. I started radiation on August 18, 1981. It was the beginning of a long battle. The radiation treatment was five days a week and it continued until November of 1981, but I did have a week of reprieve when my throat was so sore I refused treatment.

Fortunately, the radiation worked and now after some thirty years I have not had a reoccurrence. I have often told people it frustrated my enemies but my friends and family were grateful. And I was and am most thankful to God, the prayers of believers, and the doctors for the healing.

Most of my life was free of any major medical detours, with the exception of the larynx cancer in the 1980's. However, while in Pennsylvania and employed at Messiah Village, I had two major medical issues.

The first episode in 1997 was an unexpected appendix operation that started with what I thought was stomach flu but it got so painful I ended up in the Harrisburg General Hospital. Following exploratory surgery, they informed me I had a "perforated appendix." The best I could figure it was the old fashioned term of "burst" appendix.

The doctor informed me they had not sutured me and I had to stay in the hospital for a week. They changed my surgical dressing every time the nurses changed their shifts, and it was a procedure I would not wish on anyone. I did note it left a really strange scar since the surgeon sewed me up lying in my bed at the hospital the day before I was released. It was obvious this physician was not a plastic surgeon. I'll share later a fall out of this operation.

My supervisor and fellow employees from Messiah Village had visited me in the hospital and the women told me that my supervisor, Linford Good, thought I might not make it. Even my wife said I didn't look very good right after the operation. Well, I recovered and went about my business.

A second medical detour occurred in 1998 when I slipped on a golf course in California while visiting our family over the Christmas/New Year season. Our son in law, Bob, and our grandson, Bryce, went golfing with me. It was just after a rain and there was some slippery mud on the course. Just after warning Bryce about the condition of the course, I slipped and fell hard. I first thought it was just a sprain, but checking it out at the hospital in California, the x-ray revealed a torn ligament in my knee.

An incident at the hospital emergency area helped temper my pain. A hospital employee came out and looking at the people sitting there glanced at me. I was wearing a sweatshirt from my alma mater, Messiah College, that only had one word on it: *Messiah.*

The young man who was taking in patients in the emergency ward said, "You are the Messiah and we haven't taken you in?" Well, a lady next to me with a child obviously sick with a nasty cold, interrupted what was clearly meant as a pun and joke and loudly proclaimed, "I was here before him!" He took her in, winked at me, and then when we finally went in, he informed me he was Jewish and we had a hearty laugh. So it was a really funny episode on a New Year's Eve weekend.

I returned to Pennsylvania and this time, in the Holy Spirit hospital in Camp Hill, Pennsylvania, I had my knee repaired. It was a painful process and the physical therapy was difficult but I had good help and support. The physical therapy was so painful. I complained one day and the young man who was my therapist, pulled up his pant leg. He had a similar scar. He informed me some day in the future I would be grateful for this pain. He was right. Even today I have full use of my knee without any major issues.

I had a very nasty scar from the appendix operation I had in 1997 while living in Pennsylvania. And in 2000 I was getting a noticeable stomach paunch. I thought it was just a part of getting older, but our daughter in law, Carol, said, "Dad that is not a normal tummy paunch, please have it checked," so I did. It was diagnosed as an incisional hernia. I had it repaired in the Riverside, California Kaiser hospital. It was supposed to be a one night deal, but I ended up in the hospital three nights, due to an infection and tearing of the skin when the bandage was removed. I endured a lot of pain. I returned home and healed.

About two years later I had a call from the surgeon, Doctor Baril, and she informed me that the mesh piece placed internally to cure my hernia was on recall! I was stunned and replied, "Say what?" She quickly said, "Now don't be alarmed, we aren't going to take it out." She continued, "I just have to inform you and if you ever have trouble we will pay all costs." It was not a word of comfort. I called her back the next day after a fretful night and asked questions and she assured me to just forget it with no limitations on exercise or anything. She advised me only one in a thousand seemed to have a problem. I just hope I am not one of those every thousand patients! Well it has been more than ten years now and I have no issue; other than knowing I am living with a recalled part. I always thought of recalls as auto parts.

The most recent detour was in June, 2011 during my interim pastoral stint at Cedar Grove Brethren in Christ church. I had a gall bladder attack and ended up in the Lewistown, Pennsylvania hospital for nine days. There was pancreatitis and some heart fibrillation which complicated the surgery. It was with gratitude that once again there was quick healing and a return to normal activities.

I survived these detours, but it is a reminder that I am getting older.

Chapter 29

Senior Adventures

Shortly after leaving Messiah Village I was involved in a memorial service for my friend and former colleague, Erwin Thomas. After the service, Bishop Craig Sider, son of my former colleague Roy Sider and a friend, greeted me and asked how things were going. I asked if he wanted a nice response or the truth. He asked for the truth. I left him know I was unemployed and feeling discouraged. He then asked me if I wanted to take an interim pastorate. I asked some questions about the prospect. Shortly after that encounter I was invited to take a four month interim pastoral role at the Skyline View Brethren in Christ church just east of Harrisburg, Pennsylvania. My time there proved to be a real serendipity.

The Skyline View Brethren In Christ Interim

It was refreshing to be back in pastoral ministry. It was also a new beginning for me to use video along with preaching. There was a young man skilled in using computer power point. He did enjoy slipping in cartoons when I did not expect it. I soon learned to use power point and control the operation myself. I also had a wedding for a black couple that involved another culture. The former pastor John Reitz helped me with the marriage counseling format and materials.

And I enjoyed working with the church board. I was challenged to help them move on and to guide them since a new church planting was taking place fairly close. I thought it was most helpful to have a definite time period as interim and this model was a good one for me.

After finishing at Skyline View I started negotiations with the New Guilford Brethren in Christ church in Franklin County not too far from where I grew up in Waynesboro, Pennsylvania. I was serving the church as a consultant and being considered for a position as their interim pastor.

The Riverside Brethren in Christ Interim

In the midst of those negotiations, Marlene and I received a call from a church board member in Riverside, California, wondering if we would be open to do an interim pastoral assignment at the Riverside, California Brethren in Christ church. I had talked earlier with Bishop John A. Brubaker, my friend and former colleague, who was now the Pacific Conference bishop. He wasn't sure he had any openings at the time that I might want. I knew Bishop John was working with the Riverside church and at the time they were not interested in inviting anyone. So in my response to the phone call from Riverside, I advised the Riverside church to call the Bishop.

We eventually had communication from the Bishop indicating that Riverside had changed courses and now wanted to issue an invitation for us to go to Riverside. My wife was excited. It would get us back to California and a church was paying for our move. If you knew my wife's sense of frugality, this was the best of all options.

We made a trip to interview for the position and Bishop Brubaker that evening informed the group that it was an interview that he had a hunch was settled before it started. We found a rental house on that same trip in the next city, Moreno Valley. We moved to Riverside in the summer of 2000. We agreed to serve as interim pastor at Riverside for one year. Both we and the group there found our times together mutually satisfying and fulfilling.

Marlene and I were asked to take another year and we agreed. About half way through 2002 we sensed that Riverside needed a younger and more aggressive pastor to lead them into the future. Besides, we wanted to locate where we would be closer to our two children and grandchildren. Reluctantly, we informed the Riverside church that we would be leaving in the summer of 2002.

Farewell at Riverside Church, 2002

2002 the Move to Pinon Hills, California

Our daughter, Bernice, observed how happy and fulfilled we were and one time said, "Dad, you are really backing into retirement." I asked what she meant and she pointed out how I had been taking these pastoral interims which didn't tie us down as much as a long term pastorate and we were taking some time to be with family. I agreed and so it is my sense that, in many ways, we are still backing into retirement, whatever *retirement* means.

Many people have different concepts about retirement, but that I'll leave to other writers. For Marlene and me, it means we make decisions that are best for the people we serve and for us. It is a balance every person or couple has to discern and make choices that are right.

We started looking at Upland Manor, our Regional Conference Church Retirement Apartments, as a possible location after our time at Riverside. But our son questioned us "moving into a place with all the older people." I informed him a number of them were close to our age. At any rate, he encouraged us to look for land and have a house built.

To our great joy, we discovered some available real estate in a place we often passed through on the way to our son's home. In Pinon Hills, California we found a two and a half acre plot, had a house built and our financial obligations were less than if we had moved to Upland Manor. Once again my wife was a "happy camper!" We were surely blest.

So in September of 2002 we moved into the new house we had built. Marlene and I really had a great deal of pleasure working on this project. It was exciting to make choices and watch the project come to completion. We have lived in the high desert for over a decade as of this writing, and often remark how much we enjoy this area. We have also had a lot of fun landscaping our property and have more than enough area to work on the rest of our lives on earth. We were blest to buy land and get our house built at a time just before land values and building costs escalated beyond anyone's expectations for this area of California.

When we built in 2002, Marlene's brother wondered why in the world we would want to live in the high desert. He remarked it was just because land was less expensive. We agreed, but by 2002 this area had also become expensive and while we had no intention of seeing any value in increased equity, it has been an unexpected development.

However, with the economy one never knows what might happen, because by 2009 property values had dropped dramatically. All we know is we were led to make good decisions at a good time. For this we are grateful to God and our family and friends.

We moved to Pinon Hills in September of 2002. A group of people from the Riverside Brethren helped us load a U-Haul truck and moved us from Moreno Valley to our new house. We had a pizza party on the back porch and it was a day of celebration. Marlene and I were truly happy to have this location and beautiful new house.

We were not really aware that the area is smog free and not as much wind as in adjacent areas of the high desert. It is on the north slope of the San Gabriel Mountains. The local chamber of commerce calls it "where the desert meets the mountains." That is literally true. We have numerous juniper trees, sage, Joshua trees and other native plants and shrubs on our property.

One interesting involvement was meeting our new neighbors. Just south up the hill in the third house on the west live a couple, Gene and Sharon Waggoner. They kept an eye on our house while it was being built. After we moved in, they invited us to take regular morning walks with them and we did that for the first couple years. We also went on a camping trip with them. It is their fifth marriage and so we were learning about a different kind of family life and a variety of beliefs beyond what we had witnessed before. We still keep our ties as neighbors and help each other when convenient.

Our neighbors to the east and the only neighbor whose land is adjacent to us is a story. We first met Bill and Beverly Queen by going to their house as total strangers and knocking on their door. It was just after we had our land in escrow. We wanted to meet our closest neighbors. They were most cordial and invited us in and began to tell us how much they loved the area, the weather, the size of property, the wonderful four seasons, and so forth. They sounded like sales people for the chamber of commerce. But when I said we would be neighbors, Bill immediately changed and told us of possible noise from the highway to the north and the smell of horses to the southeast.

As a matter of fact, he left a note on our car subsequent to the visit informing us of other properties available. But we had already decided on this land. Then when we had the corners marked, we discovered our property line went right down the middle of his driveway. He admitted he might be using some of our land. He used our land to walk his dogs and had hoped no one would ever locate on this land.

About six months later we decided to erect a fence. He had told us earlier he hoped we would never put up a fence. Well, as it turned out when we were ready to have the fence erected, I would be away. Incidentally, he had tried to offer a lease plan, a purchase plan, and finally offered to pay for the fence if we gave him six feet of land at one end but no paper work. We declined. One morning we were out walking and we met Bill. I told him I would be away when the fence men came and whatever he and Marlene worked out would be fine. He queried me as to whether this was really agreeable with me. He had no idea what I had just done. Marlene is much more firm than me on such matters.

When I returned home he informed me I was married to an "intense woman." I had to hide my smile. In fact, Marlene and the fence men had to tell Bill he needed to remove a fair amount of concrete that he had laid on our property. To his credit he had it broken up and removed in a month as Marlene had told him he would need to have it done. It took some time but now we are cordial neighbors.

Several years later we met Belinda Munoz. She was walking their dog and joined us walking with Gene and Sharon. We soon met her husband Robert and then met their autistic son Steven. We also learned they had a married son Robert, Jr. living in Tennessee. Robert, Jr. was beginning a new ministry named, GOD, Global Overseas Development, and a new missions venture.

We became very close friends with the Munoz family. About a year after we started walking, Belinda was diagnosed with ALS (Arterial Lateral Scleroses), more popularly known as Lou Gehrig's disease. It was very hard news. She confided in us even before she shared it with her extended family. Robert asked if I would be his pastor. They are warm friends and such generous people. We have had them in our home several times and they have invited us to their place. We also looked after each other's properties when we were gone.

They have given us a large cactus made of horseshoes, a pair of antique wheels from a Mexican cart, and later two mining cars from an old gold mine. We also have two old bathtubs they gave us that we use as planters. They bought a house in Tennessee and live close to their married son and two very young granddaughters. Robert casts fish and paints them for people and organizations. His work is literally all over the world. He is a really gifted artist but very humble and unassuming. Just as I was finishing these stories, we heard that Belinda passed away. We will share in her memorial service here in California.

Also out walking, we met a Korean couple, Bob and Jeanie Nam. We walked with them for many months and they would have us into their home. They in turn introduced us to another couple Jun and Sonja Kim. We still see them occasionally.

The Mennonite Insurance Board

Shortly after our move to Pinon Hills I received a phone call that was an invitation to serve on the Board of the Mennonite Insurance Services centered in Fresno, California. It was an opportunity that has been a fulfilling pursuit for me. For the first time in my life of sitting on more boards and committees than I could list, I was offered an honorarium for attending the meetings and all expenses paid including some spousal expenses. But beyond that, it was intriguing to learn the world of insurance while being a part of a non-profit agency serving Anabaptist churches and families.

One factor of special interest was a claim on a policy held by the Brethren in Christ church in Ontario, California, which had a devastating fire. I was not aware of the tension between the insurance manager and the local pastor. But when I asked if I should excuse myself, the chairman informed me it would not be necessary. The Board paid the claim, the pastor eventually left and so it was not an issue. I have now served on the board for over nine years. I have made friends with the members of the board and have enjoyed meeting with them and hearing investment and accounting specialists give us direction. It is a new world for me and I find it fascinating.

The Cross-Country Interim Pastoral Adventure 2002-2003

Ken Letner was a cherished young man and friend during my years of ministry. In late summer of 2002 just as we were moving to Pinon Hills, California, I was invited to serve as interim pastor of the Cedar Grove Brethren in Christ church near Mifflintown, Pennsylvania. The call came from Warren Hoffman and I said, "Warren, have you forgotten, we now live in California." He wanted me to fly east every four weeks and spend a week including two weekends, but eventually I agreed to fly east every six weeks and spend two weekends.

Ken Letner, who had been elected bishop of that area, still lived there and had his office nearby. I would stay in his home and spend a week including the two weekends. I accepted and it was a nine month commitment that proved to be a "chairos" time for me. It was a serendipity.

I began in October of 2002. I had the counsel and wisdom of Ken Letner, the former pastor and now the bishop. I learned to know the staff comprised of three full time gifted people, Craig Zent, Tony Rohrer and Debby Bench. The church secretary, Gail Haubert, was also very supportive. They enabled me with their trust and support to serve them and the congregation in this unique cross-country adventure. They had two Sunday morning services, one traditional and the second contemporary. It was a stretch for me to shift styles and preach to two different groups but one congregation.

Pastor Ken had built the congregation to become one of the larger Pennsylvania churches in our denomination. I learned a lot and was really fulfilled to counsel with the staff and share from my pastoral heart and many years of church experience. Much of the pain of being let go from Messiah Village was healed with this great affirmation and opportunity to minister.

At the annual business meeting someone questioned the expense of having this "interim pastor" from California. Anticipating such a question, I had asked the chairman if I could speak in case that question came up. I then noted that in the files Pastor Ken had figured out it would cost less to fly me in every six weeks than pay a full salary and mileage for a retired minister from Messiah Village. A man with a sense of humor asked if I ever heard of "Ollie's" a variety store in Pennsylvania. I acknowledged I had. Well he said then you are "good stuff cheap" which was the store slogan. I assured him I hoped that was true. With a chuckle the business resumed.

While at Cedar Grove I learned to know many of the members, visited in some homes and shared in the family life of the Letners. The confidences that people shared and the dynamics of congregational life rekindled my love of the parish ministry. As Ken pointed out it was likely a once in a life time event but it seemed to work for the congregation and me. In the winter of that year Ken treated me to a Penn State football game with a group from the church. It was a freezing but fascinating time. Winter underwear and double socks made it a tolerable event.

One week I was there he made homemade sauerkraut, which was a new experience for me to observe. And I enjoyed eating it which his wife prepared so well. During those visits to the east I was able to connect with some of my former friends in Pennsylvania and I thoroughly enjoyed this unexpected but transforming involvement.

Marlene was with me when we completed the time in June of 2003. The congregation affirmed her. I recall Craig Zendt saying, after meeting Marlene, "the church had hired the wrong person." They presented me with a very nice golf club and we ended a very special time.

During the next eight years we settled into Pinon Hills and continued our visits to Riverside where we retained our church membership and ties to the Brethren in Christ.

However Marlene had discovered a small independent Lutheran church just east of Phelan, California, and we have often attended church there when we chose not to drive the 100 mile round trip to Riverside. I also wanted to give the new pastor, Paul Schletewitz, at Riverside an opportunity, without me present, to bond with the congregation.

In terms of ministry, I met every two weeks with Eric Sythoff who was planting a new church in Riverside, California. I also spent time once every two weeks with Steve Airth who was planting a new church in Ontario, California. Those were good times for all three of us.

We also spent more time with our children and grandchildren.

Evergreen Lutheran Church

I noted above, Marlene found a small congregation just east of us. We attend there when we are at our home in Pinon Hills. It has been a joy to reconnect with Jake and Jeannie Stern, former acquaintances from our years in Upland, California. I have often met with Jake for breakfasts in which we share our journeys. This has been a good experience. It has been enriching to have Jake share his joys and disappointments. We both like to reminisce and update our present experiences of life. And two other men both named, John, have joined us on some mornings. It is a good humor group and a nice diversion for the week. I think of it as laughing with the Lutherans.

Marlene and I have also found some new friends at this church. A small group usually meets for lunch after the morning worship and we have often joined them. We have become a part of this congregation in its life. The pastor, Christian Andrews, has asked me to fill the pulpit on some occasions when he is away. We enjoy this circle of friends as a part of our life in the high desert.

"Uh Oh" Experience

One summer morning we had gone to the dentist and, upon returning home, discovered thieves had kicked in our front door and stole our printer/copier, television, stereo, any cash they could find, numerous tools, all the valuables in the bedroom, plus some other sundry items. The sheriff was called and he indicated it was likely kids seeking drug money.

I was puzzled why they would take a croquet set and leave my more valuable golf clubs. The sheriff informed me these kinds of persons will likely not become brain surgeons. I got the message.

It left us feeling exposed but we picked up and went on. We took our grandsons camping the next week.

Upon returning home we secured our property and have not had any intrusions since.

In September of 2004, Dale and Marian Bomberger came and we took them to Yosemite National Park. Dale always has a droll sense of humor. His wife was really impressed with the natural beauty of the Yosemite Valley and the large redwoods. She repeatedly remarked about these features and asked Dale what he thought. Dale said, "It looks like a lot of dirt and rocks to me." We all laughed and Marian's usual response was "Oh Dale!"

One of the times we always enjoyed was with a group at Riverside playing pinochle. It involved Dennis and Dorcas Good, Randy and Barbara Barkley, Don and Jan Jenkins. Dorcas Good had instigated this group, and we had really great times playing cards and then sharing in a meal. Our friend, Don Jenkins, passed away in 2007 and so the group changed and eventually we discontinued meeting.

The Ontario Brethren in Christ Interim

In late 2004 I was invited to take an interim pastorate at the Ontario Brethren in Christ Church in Ontario, California. I accepted and informed them it would be one year.

We made the eighty-mile round trip at least three Sundays a month and I would be in the office at least once a week. Again it was a fulfilling time. The group had experienced a church fire and then the pastor left suddenly amidst some conflict that involved the staff and the bishop. As mentioned earlier, Bishop Perry Engle was my wife's nephew. When they invited me he informed them I was his uncle but they wanted me anyway. It was my pleasure to assist them to resolve the levels of conflict. Ralph and Joan Winger, the former bishop and wife, attend there, so they were supportive and helpful.

We got beyond the conflict and prepared the way for a new pastor. It was a good year and I enjoyed working with some persons I had known over the years along with some very gifted new persons. It was a church in transition in a neighborhood that now consisted mostly of people of Mexican descent. So it took a different kind of pastor for the days ahead.

During this year I continued meeting with Eric Sythoff and Steve Airth who were church planters I noted before. Bishop Perry Engle had me consulting with these two men. They provided me a challenge and I was still learning more about church planting after all the years I had been involved.

Fifty Years of Marriage

Glenn Ginder called the year before we celebrated fifty years of marriage. He proposed we, two couples, take a cruise together to celebrate our 50-year marriages. It eventuated in a cruise to Alaska. Glenn and Joyce, as noted earlier had been attendants at our wedding and we both were close to celebrating 50 years of marriage. So in August, 2005 we boarded the Oosterdam, cruise ship of the Holland America line. We had a wonderful trip up the Pacific Ocean from Seattle, Washington north via Ketchikan, Sitka and waterways into Glacier Bay, Alaska. We did have some thirty-foot waves on the trip north but the four of us were good sailors with no sickness and we all enjoyed this memorable celebration of our marriages.

Then, on August 30th, 2006, we decided we wanted to celebrate the actual date with just our children and grandchildren. So we gathered at our son's place and had a great time of food and memories. Our son and daughter had planned the event with a set of slides from our past which was a great time of laughter and blessing. Marlene and I had a special weekend at a bread and breakfast place, Strawberry Inn in Idyllwild, California. We have had a great marriage and it continues.

Don and Marlene at Grand Canyon, 2010

The High School Class Reunions

The boy who had become a bishop was often a mystery to his classmates. So it was fun to return to two high school class reunions. The first was of my senior year of high school at what was then Messiah Academy. In 2004 the class had a 50-year reunion in Grantham, Pennsylvania. It was fun to visit with people who had known me fifty years ago. There were some of course that we had kept in touch with but others we had not seen in fifty years. It was amazing that out of a class of fifty students, there had only been four deaths. There was some footage of film of the class trip to Washington, DC in 1954 that was beyond funny. We also had time to just visit, share snacks, special meals and remember those not present.

One amazing couple was our class advisors, Isaiah and Doris Harley, and they are still living in 2010. And a Messiah College professor who had lost two wives was now married to one of our classmates. Dr. Kenneth Hoover had married Gladys Lehman and now he was one of our class spouses! He is also still living. Getting reconnected was rewarding and gave us reason to be thankful.

The other class reunion occurred five years later. I had lost contact with my high school class of Waynesboro, Pennsylvania. In 2009 they had a 55-year reunion. The year before, we had met with eleven members of the class in the home of Sandy Fisher and planned with Carolyn Carter. They had a number of articles, such as drama programs, old photos, yearbooks, etc. and with this small group I was privileged to recall the good times of 1950-1953.

It was very interesting to meet these people since most of them I had not seen in over fifty years. I was especially pleased to meet a former friend, Tom Cross, who was our basketball star in those years. He and his wife, Lynne, now live in Texas, and we enjoyed visiting with them. We met at the Waynesboro Country Club for the main event.

The Yuma Winters

In the summer of 2005, John and Pat Kershaw, a couple we had befriended years before at Upland, California, called and invited us to go camping in Yuma, Arizona for two months in January and February, 2006. We had never camped that long at a stretch. However, it appealed to us, so we joined them and we had a wonderful two months reuniting with our friends and trying a new lifestyle in the winter months of 2006. We were now *snowbirds* and discovered a whole new set of friends mostly from the northern tier states and many Canadians.

During our second year, 2007, we moved from a park called Sun Vista to Mountain Cactus Ranch. In December of 2007, Marlene and I decided to purchase a park model which is a mobile unit that is now permanent, and we sold our recreational fifth wheel. John and Pat had a motor home and in the winter of 2010 they sold their unit. So now Marlene and I extend our winter visits on our own. John and Pat do come to visit. Beginning in 2007 our annual practice has been to head to Yuma in late October and stay until March or even mid-April. We usually return home for Christmas. We will also return to California for any family concerns or celebrations. It is only about a four and a half hour drive.

We have learned to know new friends from Canada and northern states. We enjoy the relaxed lifestyle and of course the warmer winter weather. As I mentioned earlier, Marlene really enjoys crafts, games and exercise programs. We enjoy card games with other couples. I play golf, and we both got involved in shuffleboard and sometimes pool.

One couple from Canada, Mac and Joyce Van Sickle, play cards with us about once a week while in Yuma.

They invited us to visit their very large farming operation and we did in the summer of 2009. They have three sons and it was fascinating to visit them in their home setting about fifty miles north of Medicine Hat, Alberta. We were there during the harvest time and had a ride on their very large combine and tractor trailer that hauls the grain to local elevators. We also visited two couples in North Dakota on that same trip.

We became very good friends with Irene Mechelke, a widow lady who lives in the park all year round. She keeps us apprised of the hot summers. She also keeps an eye on our *Cactus Cabin*. The summer of 2012 she called and told us our carport was blown away in a severe windstorm. We share back and forth and she has helped us with several projects. She is a friend indeed.

Another benefit of travelling to Yuma was to reconnect with a friend we had met during our Upland years. Linda Hughes, a missionary with Wycliffe Translators, who lives between our place in California and Yuma. We have renewed our relationship by way of E-mails and her newsletters. She invited us to see where she lives and that has been a good contact.

Sawmill Canyon

One of the projects we have enjoyed is helping our son and his family who decided to build a family retreat house in a place called Sawmill Canyon. It is located in the Tehachapi Mountains about eighty miles northwest of where we live. It is a remote location back on an unpaved road about five miles and at 5,000 feet elevation. There was no water or electricity. Wild horses roam the area and more recently some imported wild hogs have been seen and essentially eliminated.

At first Bruce thought he could dig his own well, but after a couple of experiments, which we had fun trying, a professional well digger has put in a pump and there is plenty of good fresh water. We helped Bruce set a 5,000-gallon water tank at a high elevation and dig trenches between the well and the proposed property site. Bruce has designed a solar pump that operates the well pump.

One episode Marlene is proud of was being hoisted to the top of the water tank, which I was afraid of doing. Bruce said, "Mom, we can do this!" She has always believed him, so the two of them installed a floating switch inside the tank which was no small feat. I did help get her up and off the tank. We have also helped clear land. It is such a beautiful and scenic area, we just love seeing this development. There is an old barn and a ranch house that may be razed but they serve now as a base for operations. It is a fun time to assist in this adventure.

In the fall of 2011 two small bear cubs were spotted in the canyon. The basement and walls are complete. The windows and roof will soon be completed so it is coming along real well.

Chapter 30

Back East

I received another phone call from Warren Hoffman in the winter of 2009. He invited me to come to the General Conference and speak about the decades we were involved in church growth.

So we returned to Pennsylvania to address the General Conference of 2010 that I previously led as General Secretary. It was a unique opportunity and I shared my speech.

I have been encouraged to include that speech and thus I have added it as **Appendix C**.

At the close of my speech, Warren asked me to stay at the podium and he read a generous citation and handed me a plaque naming me General Secretary Emeritus of The Brethren in Christ Church, North America. It was a total surprise and an honor. I asked for only one response. He granted it and I had my wife stand since she deserved this honor as much as I did. Below is the citation which summarizes my career in church work.

Citation presented at the 121ˢᵗ General Conference
of the Brethren in Christ Church in North America
July 10, 2010

RAYMOND DONALD SHAFER, the Brethren in Christ Church has been greatly blessed by the leadership you have given us over many years.

Your leadership qualities became apparent when you were a student at Messiah College. The school's yearbooks show that you served as a president of student government and in numerous student organizations, often as the leader. Indeed, it almost seems that the only group that did not have your membership and leadership was the Sewing Club!

The experience you gained in leadership at Messiah College helped to prepare you for leadership in the Brethren in Christ Church. Your leadership roles included pastor of the Elizabethtown Brethren in Christ Church, Director of Sunday Schools for the denomination, Executive Director of Christian Education (another denominational agency), Bishop of the Midwest and Pacific Conferences, and the first full-time General Secretary of the Brethren in Christ Church in North America. This list fails to tell of the many other denominational and non-denominational agencies in which you served.

In all of these positions you were known as an able administrator. You were efficient and pragmatic, interested in making things happen, and in working well with colleagues to achieve the ends you sought.

You were also visionary. You could see new possibilities for the church. You understood how new organizational structures and extending our horizon would be beneficial to the denomination.

Such leadership qualities can be illustrated in various ways, including your work as Executive Director of Christian Education, one of your first denominational appointments. In this role you took the lead in merging three commissions—Sunday School, Home, and Youth—into a strong Board of Christian Education.

Your leadership qualities can also be illustrated in your role as Bishop of the Midwest and Pacific Conferences. One of the pastors then under your care claims that you were "the first bishop of the Pacific Conference to enter into church growth in a serious way." In doing so, you surrounded yourself with church growth professionals, such as John Wimber, Donald McGavern, and Peter Wagner from nearby Fuller Theological Seminary. When you accepted the leadership of the Pacific Conference, only twelve congregations existed in the Conference. Under your leadership that number increased dramatically, and the stage was set for continued church growth.

As bishop you also helped pastors to develop into viable leaders of their congregations. To accomplish this end you introduced retreats for pastors and spouses and organized seminars to which you frequently brought knowledgeable resource persons.

You are remembered with gratitude for your role as General Conference Secretary. In this position your leadership qualities, developed over the years, came to full maturity. You knew how to encourage colleagues to assist you in achieving administrative goals. You could confront when necessary, but at the same time you were concerned that confrontation did not create personal harm. You were willing to work with decisions when they went against your judgment. You did not shrink from tough challenges, as with the *Renewal 2000* restructuring, to reposition the church strongly for the future. As a denominational leader you represented us well in such organizations as the National Association of Evangelicals and the Mennonite Central Committee. In turn, such groups held you in high regard.

Not least, you strongly supported Brethren in Christ doctrine, including our position on peace, yet even here you did not hesitate to foster change, such as a new position for the church on divorce and remarriage. You initiated and led the Church through a comprehensive review and restatement of our *Articles of Faith and Doctrine.*

In all of these activities and in your personal relationships you are remembered as being generous and warm, good natured and optimistic. "To the services of the church," a colleague has recalled, "you often added a relaxing overlay of genuine good humor."

Your home life reflected these attitudes. Your love and support of your wife Marlene, and she of you, were obvious for all to see. As your children and grandchildren arrived in your home, it was clear that you cared equally for them as you did for the church. You and your family became models of what life could be in the church.

Don, the Brethren in Christ have benefited greatly by your leadership and ministry of many years. As much as anyone, you have "brought us on our way." Truly, you came among us "for such a time as this."

In honor of your inestimable service, including twenty-four years as a denominational leader, the General Conference Board of the Brethren in Christ Church in North America confers on you the honorary title of General Secretary Emeritus.

Warren L. Hoffman, Moderator
Donald F. McNiven, General Secretary

As I listened, it seemed as though I was present at my own memorial service, but thank God, the reality was I was just being blest with kind words.

Don Shafer

Another event on this same trip was to return to Elizabethtown, Pennsylvania in the summer of 2010 since the Elizabethtown Brethren in Christ church was celebrating 100 years of history. It was hard for me to believe, I was pastor there fifty years ago. So I spoke on "A Look in the Window into the Elizabethtown Church Fifty Years Ago." It was a pleasure to reminisce and meet a number of the people who were there fifty years ago. The young pastor there in 2010 was Steve Lane, a young man I mentored to some degree when we lived in Pennsylvania from 1992-2000. J. Harold Engle, my friend over the years, and a son of this congregation was instrumental in having this special arrangement.

The summer of 2010 trip also involved a "beach wedding" in Avalon, New Jersey. The event there was the marriage of my youngest niece, Katie Arbaugh, my youngest sister, Nancy's, daughter. This meant contacts with my four siblings at the wedding and in their homes following the wedding. It was especially meaningful to have extra time with my brother Sam and his wife Mary since Sam was dealing with multiple myeloma and was in the healing process after four major surgeries. It brought us together in a way that I felt was a special closeness. We prayed together for his healing and God's peace to be with him and his family.

We enjoyed times in the homes of Marlene's siblings in Pennsylvania and then in Kansas. We heard her brother Delbert had fallen. He had been living with Alzheimer's disease and now, after being in the hospital for a few days, was transferred to a long-term care facility. We had quality time with his wife, Twila, and a meal with Delbert. We had no idea that upon our return home we would have a phone call from Marlene's sister, Mary, telling us Delbert had died on July 27, 2010. It was a shock but in his condition, with memory loss and other issues, it was a blessing. It is a stark reminder of our mortality and our business of getting older.

Our daughter, Bernice, and family decided to make a move and so we helped with this event. They had not moved in sixteen years so this was a major change. In addition, they had a beloved dog, Britney, who was suffering and they finally made the hard decision to have her put to sleep. This all happened within one weekend so it was very hard. We helped them with a garage sale and took several truckloads to a local thrift store. Now they are located in the same city of South Pasadena but in a better situation. Their two children are off to university so they have an empty nest. A few weeks later we shared in the burial of Britney's ashes on our place with a small memorial stone. It is a part of making memories.

An Affirming Invitation

In late 2010 Bishop Doug Sider called and invited me to share with a group of pastors in a "Leadership Cohort" at Camp Hebron, Pennsylvania. So on March 6-7, 2011 I flew from Yuma, Arizona to Harrisburg, Pennsylvania. It was a joy to share from my life in the church with younger leaders and gifted pastors. It was especially exciting to have time with the two young bishops, Doug Sider and Nathan Yoder. It was a blessing to have this opportunity. I did perceive what one of the contemporary writers of my generation wrote, "The times they are a chang'in." I was told to get an air ticket, a motel and rental car. In my earlier days we would have been advised to get a cheap fare, find lodging and see if a friend could transport me. I really found this new freedom not too hard to handle. But the real reward was to share values from my life journey that I believe transcend any changes in time and culture.

I did find my way on Sunday morning, March 6th, to attend the Harrisburg Brethren in Christ church ministering in a cross-cultural part of the city. My friend, the pastor Woody Dalton, preached a prophetic sermon which encouraged me on the church today. Several children of parents I had worked with and friends of bygone days recognized me and we had encouraging conversations.

Cedar Grove, Second Interim

Bishop Doug Sider called in the late spring of 2011 and said he had a job for me. I informed him I was not seeking a job. He said we need you at the Cedar Grove Brethren in Christ Church. I was surprised. I asked if they still had three full time staff.

He responded there were no staff and no senior pastor. This was shocking news. He wanted me for a longer period of time, like two years. We agreed on four months.

We were informed of how the staff and senior pastor left over issues of unfaithfulness, unbelief, betrayal, accusations and a sense of ineffective leadership. It all boils down to human relationships and some sin and yet a lot of hope and challenge.

So we drove east and spent June through September of 2011 as the interim pastor. It was both a challenging and fulfilling experience. We gave the congregation our best to bring healing and hope. It was a time of renewing acquaintance from the experience nine years prior.

We also met new people and encouraged them to release any hurts and losses and move into the future with compassion and joy. It is very affirming to be able to share with others from a life of experience in the church. Marlene really connected with the deacon couple, Brad and Sandy Hershey, and especially their two young daughters. Of course, I was pleased with this. They paid us a visit in the summer of 2012 when they came as delegates to General Conference in Ontario, California, along with another deacon couple, Kim and Linda Yousey. It brought back great memories of our time at Cedar Grove.

As noted above, I had a brief stint in the hospital, but over all we sensed we prepared the congregation to move on into the future.

While there we celebrated our 55th wedding anniversary. The staff and several other volunteers hosted us to a delightful breakfast.

Don and Marlene's 55ᵗʰ Wedding Anniversary
at Cedar Grove, Pennsylvania

Chapter 31

My Brother's Death

On the first day of November 2011, I received a call that my brother had died from a deadly infection. He had been fighting cancer and was winning that battle, but this spinal infection was fatal. Marlene and I flew to Pennsylvania. This tragic event was shocking in that most of us expect our younger siblings to outlive us. Now my brother, six years younger, suddenly died when it seemed he was overcoming one of life's physical battles.

His wife, Mary, asked me to lead the memorial service. It was hard, but I wanted to do it for my brother and our family. My tribute and some notes of the memorial event are shared as a story to lift us all in a time of sorrow and grief.

Sam and Mary Shafer, author's brother and wife

A Tribute to My Brother Sam

After tributes from my three sisters' families and a tribute from Sam's family read by Laura, Sam and Mary's son Brad's wife, I shared Psalms 8 and 109. I welcomed all and noted that we meet to honor, remember my brother, and celebrate the man we all cherished.

We, each and all, make choices in life. But sometimes we can't always have our choices. If I had a choice, I would have rather honored my brother and his wife on their 50th wedding anniversary this past June 2011. As most of you know, I was hospitalized and missed that event.

But now it is my choice to accept the invitation to be here and share in a time of memories. As the family informed me, we want this to be a time of honoring my brother as the man he was. I am pleased to try to help us remember. As a matter of fact, Sam remarked, when we were together, how we keep going over the same recollections each time we gather. He was likely the best and most accurate in recalling the details of our life together. And, fortunately, we were blest with parents and grandparents, aunts, uncles, cousins and friends that gave us these precious memories.

Sam and I started life together. He came as a gift to me, my only biological brother when I was six years old. My first memories are:

We slept together—he tells me we actually put a string down the middle of the bed to keep us in our own places.

We played together—trains and bikes and later cars with dad, uncles Ralph and Russell.

We worked together—paperboys and lawns and sanding cars.

We went to the farm together—our uncle Paul and aunt Maggie and cousins.

We went camping together—the accident, of a fender bender when I tried to open a bag of potato chips for breakfast. My brother and cousin abandoned me when I faced my dad upon our return.

We were raised together—good, Godly parents and a pastoral mentor, Sam Wolgemuth.

Then when Sam was only about eleven years old, I left home. I was married several years later and Sam was my best man. The one thing we both did with great wisdom, and possibly the best choice of our lives, was we both married strong, smart, stable, and sweet women. Mary and Marlene became part of our life together. We were blest. Mary and Marlene are saints compared to Sam and me. If you aren't sure about that, ask Sam's kids and grandkids. Our kids aren't here and they would obviously be biased, but Sam's family knows the truth.

Then our pathways changed. Sam became a good, successful, and respected business man. I became a pastor. During those years I learned something as the elder brother. Our story is in Luke chapter 15 of the Bible and the elder brother is the greatest sinner of the two. I had only one real responsibility with Sam and that was to love my brother. You see, somehow I thought as the older brother, I needed to watch over my three sisters and brother, but they all made it clear over the years that they really didn't need my oversight!

Let me capsulate my memories of Sam.

He was a man of love and loyalty. He loved his wife of over fifty years and loved his two children, Carol and Brad, their spouses, Lonn and Laura, and especially the grandchildren, Julia, Lena, William, and Samantha. Sam loved life and labored with zeal.

Sam was a manager and leader. And you all know about Adams County Auto Parts and the other stores he founded and led to eminent success. He and Mary have done well as business people in Gettysburg. I do want to share one story of my brother's business mind matched by his generosity. When we sorted through my Dad's papers following his demise, we found invoices not turned in. Sam tore them up and then said to me these guys will not be at my viewing.

Sam was also a husband and father. He would often remark and especially in recent years. "It's all about family." And he practiced that with his kind and generous ways. There is a story of an early vacation when we went on a boat trip. I offered to fill the boat with fuel and soon the toll on the pump was more than I had in my wallet. He enjoyed telling me he was taking care of it.

The reasons so many of us are here today is due to Sam's numerous families. He had his immediate and extended family. He had his marina and boating family. He had his Napa Auto Parts family. He had a Masonic and Shriner family. And he had his Gettysburg community family.

Sam was a family man. In the past decades Sam and Mary often hosted our family reunions either at their home or at their boat. When the family became larger we went to Lewes, Delaware for a family gathering. He hosted Marlene and me, family and friends as part of their Great American Loop trip. And beyond any human planning we made trips to Pennsylvania the last four summers and each summer enjoyed some special times together. And the last two summers Sam and Mary invited some cousins to share in family gatherings. In short he was a brother beloved.

And I admired his attitude and fight with this unexpected illness and attack on his body. I want to share a very personal side of my brother. When he informed me in the summer of 2009 that he had a serious diagnosis I prayed hard. And we had prayer in his home in 2010 for which I asked permission. Mary informed me if I hadn't prayed she would have asked me. But my brother made my day when he called me in the hospital when I missed their anniversary and said, "I am praying for you brother."

I want to share a prayer I wrote when Mary called and asked for some "heavy duty prayer" not knowing he was dying.

Prayer for my Brother, Sam—November 1, 2011

It's four in the morning and we heard the warning.
Mary called and it is time for heavy duty prayer and we
    are aware.
So here I am a praying and calling on the Lord for your
    healing.
We heard you are fighting a serious infection and so
We pray for the doctors and nurses inspection;
We pray for the ceasing of pain and for speedy recovery.
In the long lonely hours of hospital stay we can only
    pray.
And we would ask for you and Mary to experience God's
    peace and presence.
Times like these are always hard and I want to ask
    why???
And there seems to be no answer no matter how hard
    we cry.
But I do believe in the love of God and his promise of
    care,
So here is a plea for you to experience our promise of
    prayer.
Our fervent hope is for you to find freedom from pain
    and headed for healing,
In the midst of minds and hearts that are reeling.
We ask God to restore your body and bring you relief
    and restoration.

Your sisters and I and your family, for sure, are hoping for normalization.

Let me just say a few things about death and end with words of hope and life.
The reality is we all deal with death. One of my favorite authors, Walter Wangerin, wrote a book about "Turning Mourning into Dancing." He describes four deaths we all face.

1. The first death was in the Garden of Eden when the first humans sinned and in the *fall* we all now face death.
2. The second death is one of broken relationships. And in that sense we have all been dying to some degree.
3. The third death is our human death, which is why we are here today to remember.
4. The fourth death is a choice to leave God and go on our own. And therein is our hope. God sent his Son, Jesus Christ and for those who believe in God there is hope as evidenced by the resurrection of his Son and our Savior Jesus Christ.

And so on this day of memories let us take hope. My brother believed in the things that make a difference: Love, Family, Work, and Celebration of Life.

My Three Sisters

One of the advantages of travelling east was to reconnect with my siblings. As you noted above we had made a contact with my brother each time we were in Pennsylvania. I also arranged contacts with my sisters.

As we travelled across country, we were always invited by my sister, Nancy, and her husband, Harry, to visit with them. We had some really nice times. Nancy always arranges good meals and she usually has her friends, Angie and Loren, formerly from Pennsylvania, join us. We enjoy playing games and updating on our families.

We have also visited with Doris and her husband Danny near Hanover. Doris has entertained us with good food and keeps us up to date with her two children, Daniel and Ann, since they have now left home and have their own families.

My oldest sister Thelma and her husband Bill live in Laurel, Delaware and we made trips there to see their lovely house and setting not far from the Atlantic Ocean. Since Bill is a retired air force officer he can fly free. Thus they have visited us the last two summers and we have had two great trips together.

In 2011 we made a trek north in California taking in the scenic Pacific highway. We made a stop at the Hearst Castle and enjoyed a lengthy drive through the Redwoods in northern California. Bill treated us with a visit to the John Steinbeck museum in Salinas, California. My sister gave me John Steinbeck's book, *The Grapes of Wrath,* as a birthday gift on that trip. I knew about it, so I read it with new interest,

Then in 2012, Thelma and Bill came west again and we travelled through Arizona with stops in Yuma, Tucson, Tombstone, Globe, Sedona, Monument Valley, the Grand Canyon and parts of the famous Route 66. It has been a special joy to reconnect with my oldest sister and enjoy life together in retirement. We reminisce and enjoy life together in a way beyond our beginnings.

Hopefully my youngest sister will get west when they discontinue their working careers. We do enjoy these times together.

Chapter 32

The Journey is the Destination

Well it has been a good journey of seventy-six years and counting. As a matter of fact, I think, in many ways, I am the same boy even though by age I have now become one of the older men sometimes called "seniors."

I like the saying that we have no choice about growing older but we don't have to grow up. I often think of a gospel song that was sung when I was a boy and young man at our love feasts and at some of the local church meetings. It summarizes my outlook on life and expresses the desires of my heart. I have tried to live by it and want to finish my life on earth with this sentiment.

It was a song from the Brethren in Christ hymnal of 1935, ninth printing, 1961 hymn number 509 . . . and it is the theme of my life.

I would be true for there are those who trust me;
I would be pure for there are those who care;
I would be strong for there is much to suffer;
I would be brave for there is much to dare.

I would be friend of all, the foe, the friendless;
I would be giving and forget the gift;
I would be humble, for I know my weakness;
I would look up, and laugh, and love, and lift!

I would LOOK UP, and LAUGH, and LOVE, and LIFT!
(capitals are mine)

Chapter 33

I Believe in Relationships

A paper I wrote in recent years was prompted by my friend John Arthur Brubaker who gave us the book "This I Believe" which contains the personal philosophies of men and women across the years. I wrote my own as follows:

> It is a fact that no one lives alone. We each and all have been born due to a relationship. And we will relate to people in order to function in society.
>
> On the one hand, some are more blest than others to experience bonding and closer relationships from birth. It would seem a person who has received the gift of being in healthy relationships in their childhood has a better chance to develop into a healthy human being.
>
> On the other hand, persons deprived or isolated from others tend to suffer in many ways. Those who have experienced abuse or negative relationships early on in life seem to have an uphill struggle to enter into healthy relationships. Thus the whole arena of needy personalities, co-dependence, addictive natures, and a whole mine field of psychological disorders are potential hazards in relationships. But some have overcome these and developed rewarding relationships.
>
> I believe we thrive on relationships. We come to trust and depend on family and friends for meaning. I believe that love is the basis for all relationships. And I would rather take the risk of investing myself in relationships

and all that may cost than the alternative. To love and be loved is a source of contentment for any person. I believe if persons will discipline themselves to think of others as essential to fulfillment it will pay dividends. In relationships we love in order for the other person to find freedom and fulfillment. And in giving ourselves to others we find ourselves. No wonder that Jesus said the greatest commandment is to love God with all our heart, soul, and mind and to love others as ourselves. We were created to live in relationships.

I was very fortunate to have parents who loved me, a pastor who related to me, and extended family that affirmed me. I also had teachers, mentors, and friends who gave themselves to relate to me, thus enabling me to mature. I have found friends who gave me space and yet offered me the risk of being intimately trusted. And all this has led me to believe in relationships.

While no one seems to understand why certain people find spouses or friends that develop into lifelong commitments and relationships, we know it happens. I was fortunate to find a relationship with a spouse who has loved and trusted and been a loyal companion for over 56 years. So you might expect me to believe in relationships.

Admittedly, relationships can hurt us. It is possible to experience betrayal in relationships. It is likely that in every relationship there will be some form of conflict. Certainly, I have experienced some disappointment in a few relationships and sadly lost a few friends along life's journey. But given the profound blessing of all the relationships that I have experienced with children, youth, and adults, I have determined to build relationships and trust in others. It is a better way to grow older, loving and laughing in relationships than to hold grudges and find fault in others. So I choose to believe in taking the risk of relationships.

Epilogue

The summary of my memoirs came in a dream during Holy Week of 2011. I usually don't pay much attention to my dreams. However, this short explanation of my life came in a meeting I was attending. The statement seemed to have some merit. In this dream I was informed by a former colleague how I had written my memoirs and he liked the way I had described my life. He reported it as a summary of *"who we are, what we think, what we do, and who we become."* Well it seemed like a good short explanation of my life. As a matter of fact, I awoke, got up, went to my study and wrote down the short phrases above. I knew I had not written it anywhere quite like he stated it.

As I reflect on <u>who I am</u>, it seems to me I was a very fortunate boy who was blest with a good, functional, healthy family, a loving pastor, and church. I also found a whole host of friends. These people were all mentors who formed who I was and who I became. Indeed I was mentored from a boy in Pennsylvania beginning in 1936 and went on to serve the church in the world through 2012 and counting. (See article, *"From the Ringgold Meeting House to the General Church Office"* in the December 2011 issue of Brethren in Christ Life & Thought.) Who I am is a whole composite of the significant other people in my life. And my wife and lover Marlene has an immense impact on who I am. I am fulfilled as a father and grandfather who loves and values each time we are together as a family.

When it comes to <u>what I think</u>, I again owe it to many mentors that I mentioned in my memoir and the article I wrote for Brethren in Christ Life & Thought. My thoughts and theology were formed by those who taught me Biblical principles. My parents and grandparents gave me a solid foundation in being respectful and responsible. The teachings I received from our local church, Messiah College, my mentor Henry S. Miller and all my colleagues formed my understandings. I espoused my upbringing, so the Pietistic, Anabaptist, Wesleyan and the influence of Evangelicalism was the base of my theology. My further training at three very different seminaries, Lancaster United Church of Christ, Eastern Baptist (now Palmer), and Fuller Theological all gave me an opportunity to shape my thinking. The numerous books and authors I have read surely added to what I think. I am sure that exposure to other cultures and travel among the variety of churches and denominations gave me an expanded view of beliefs. I was not as conservative as some of my contemporaries, but neither did I become a radical liberal or the church would never have affirmed me as a leader. I do believe I was more pragmatic than philosophical or even mystical. Most of all, I was relational, thriving on events and people in my life.

As to who I did, well, as my memoir indicates, most of my life stories were centered on the church. I was challenged to serve and lead with a pastoral heart but also push for change to meet a changing world. Only the future will reveal what kind of difference my behavior made with those with whom I worked. I wrote on a name card about the time I turned 65 years of age that I am a friend, a husband, a father, a pastor, etcetera. I was mentored and I have, by God's grace, mentored others. That pretty well describes what I have done.

Finally, what can anyone say about who they become? Perhaps in my reflection and especially in recent years, it would be most affirming for me to think that I may have become a _mentor_. At least I am pleased when there are occasional calls from others to just want to talk and discuss and discern the issues of life. It would only be a way of paying a debt I owe.

For the many that mentored me it is most fulfilling to be able to share something of what I learned. As Jesus taught, "From everyone who has been given much, much will be demanded; and from the one who has been entrusted with much, much more will be asked" (Luke 12:48). So even in my past 75 years of life I purpose to give when there is opportunity. It is good to have health and strength to share with others along the pathway of life.

House in Pinon Hills, California,
Don and Marlene's Current Residence

Appendix A

The following are primary people I worked with from 1972-1984. When I became a bishop, Marlene and I were launched into relationships with Henry and Martha Ginder, Charlie and Ruth Byers, Roy and Dorothy Sider and David and Dorcas Climenhaga. We are grateful for the six years we served with them.

Then during our second term as bishop we added Harvey and Erma Sider, Alvin and Theta Book, and John and Esther Byers. Spending time in their homes and learning from them also added to our gratitude for God's servant leaders.

Then when I became General Secretary some other people enriched our lives. Harvey Sider, John Byers and I served as leaders along with Harold Chubb. I spent many times in the home of Harold and Nancy Chubb who served as Treasurer during those years.

I worked with Roger Williams, Jack and Trudy McClain, Phil Keefer, Morris Sider, Alvin and Theta Book, Frank and Lois Kipe, Lowell and Anna Jean Mann, Raymond and Sandy Sider, Doug and Charlotte Sider, Paul and Esther Snyder.

Other people from my past that had times with us are Eber and Ruth Dourte, Isaiah and Doris Harley, J. Wilmer and Velma Heisey, Glen and Linda Pierce, Dale and Ann Marie Shaw, Glenn and Kim Dalton, Mary Jane Davis-Fair, Lloyd and Lorna Hogg, Ray and Audrey Hostetter, Rodney and Lorna Sawatsky, Ray and Fern Musser, Dwight and Faye Bert, Eugene and Ruth Blacketter, Mahlon and Irene Engle, Chris and Bonnie Frey, Emerson Lesher, and Don Zook. Dr. Jesse and Fern Heise became good friends and

Jess often sent me encouraging notes. He served for many years on the boards I worked with. And many other board members and church leaders I respected. I know I will have missed names, but these come to mind after fifty plus years.

Appendix B

The following are couples assigned to churches or missions with whom I worked during 1972-1984 when I was Bishop of the Midwest and Pacific Conferences. I have listed them in alphabetical order. If I missed any it is due to poor memory because I was blest by every relationship I was privileged to share. The couples are as follows:

Herb and Ruth Anderson
Ed and Pat Ashby
John and Carmen Atwood
Jim and Lillian Bailey
Jerel and Fran Book
Verle and Marilee Brubaker
Amos and Alice Buckwalter
Bob and Mary Lou Bushnell
Fred and Caroline Carter
Norman and Muriel Channel
Art and Ella Cooper
Clyde and Olive Denney
Jesse and Wilma Dourte
LeRoy and Judy Eberly
Jim and Terry Ernst
Jin & Gladys Esh
Bruce and Sandy Finfrock
Rick and Leigh Ann Feeney
Jack and Jeanine Finley

Sam and Mary Fisher
Ron and Marilyn Freeman
John and Dorothy Freese
Glenn and Joyce Ginder
Rich and Doris Goswiller
Arthur and Anna Grove
Millard and Minnie Halderman
John and Joleen Hawbaker
Marion and Rachel Heisey
Bob and Barbara Hempy
Paul and Esther Hess
Paul and Evelyn Hill
Warren and Connie Hoffman
Sam and Charlotte Hollingsworth
Harold and Carolyn Jackson
Adolph and Evelyn Jordan
Keith and Verde Knaack
Henry and Faith Landis
Carl and Gail Lewis
Kevin and Candy Longenecker
Larry and Nancy Martin
Cal and Pat Morey
Freddy and Pat Negrete
John and Kathy Neufield
Charles and Elaine Norman
Stan and Beth Norman
Woody and Gerry Peabody
Charles and Barbara Rickel
Ed, Deanna (deceased) and Martha Rickman
Kevin and Gail Ryan
Clayton and Orpha Severn
Elbert and Arlene Smith
Glen and Miriam Smith
John and Marian Snook

Floyd and Beth Speck
Eric and Roberta Stanton
Les and Gail Steele
Aaron and Martha Stern
Ralph and Joan Wenger
Rod and Gwen White
Garland and Virginia Whittington
Keith and Edith Whitford

Appendix C

The following is the speech I was asked to give at the Brethren in Christ General Conference in July 2010. It covers a major part of my career with the Brethren in Christ Church.

"Transformation" is the theme of this conference. In many ways the life of the Brethren in Christ Church has been a process of transformation. From a predominantly rural people and culture with practices of the "plain people" of Lancaster County, Pennsylvania, we have changed to a recognized denomination among the smaller evangelical groups in our society. When I did studies at Fuller Theological Seminary in the 1970's a fellow student referred to the Brethren In Christ as a "sect." That description annoyed me and I refuted the opinion but it was a reminder of how others perceived us.

Let me begin in the early 1960's when I was privileged to enter the Brethren in Christ ministry as a young man in my mid-twenties. It was my perception that our church was on a path of becoming more connected and more concerned about reaching people for Christ. I was encouraged to associate with other pastors in the community and discovered other church families had similar traits with us. There were of course some differences.

There were obvious cultural changes. The growing antiwar sentiment in the 1960's and 1970's was a radical reversal of the stigma against the peace churches in the 1940's and 1950's. The advent of television changed our church dramatically. In our first parish we had our television upstairs since there was still some strong negative attitude toward this worldly innovation. Like the rest of America many had moved to town and in meeting other believers we had to deal with "being in the world but not of the world" in new ways.

People were experiencing the scattering of the extended family. Along with peers my marriage to a girl from Kansas meant our biological families were over a thousand miles apart. Beyond that many of our youth were marrying across church and racial lines. The Brethren in Christ also joined the ranks of broken relationships in families including divorce. So it was a time when the church had to deal with divorced members and leaders. On the positive side, our Anabaptist heritage of community life was now attractive to some people.

A major tension we faced was keeping our brotherhood heritage and church practices and, at the same time, sharing our faith and life with people we were relating to in neighborhoods at work and play.

From 1966 until 1972, just prior to becoming involved as a bishop and in church planting, it was my experience to visit our churches in North America for purposes of what we now name Congregational Life. We helped numerous congregations do self-studies about their purpose and mission. It was obvious most of our congregations were changing.

Some signs of change were church architecture and worship practices. The divided chancel at Upland, California, Carlisle Pennsylvania, and Nappanee, Indiana, were innovations for a denomination that had buildings like the Maryland Ringgold Meeting house.

It is important for me to affirm the influence gifted to me by mentors and colleagues who blest my life. My parents loved the church, introduced me to Jesus and enabled me to enjoy church, unlike some of my peers. (That was likely a residue of legalism and rigid membership regulations that I did not experience.) Sam Wolgemuth, my pastor until I left for college, modeled vision and growth. He instilled a love for Jesus and the church and had a passion for the unchurched people of the world. My teachers at Messiah College and my mentor, Henry S. Miller at Elizabethtown Brethren in Christ church molded my love and loyalty to the Brethren in Christ. Brother Miller was a man who decreased that I might increase. He was a rare model of an affirming leader who believed in me and gave me wise advice. And the challenge of my fellow bishops, especially the late Roy V. Sider, sharpened my sense of pushing out to new frontiers.

Later, in the mid 1970's training at Fuller Theological Seminary and the consultation of the late John Wimber enabled me to dream new dreams, set goals and move with passion. I owe a debt of gratitude to the people ahead of me and to those who worked with me to form ideas and ideals.

Starting new churches began in the 1950's and 1960's. As a matter of fact our church membership grew from about 5,500 to 11,000 from 1950 to 1975. By the early 1970's we were reviewing the vision and strategies for church growth.

In terms of process, before 1972 we focused on building a church facility, then employing a pastor and, with subsidy help and sometimes people, we urged the formation of a new congregation. Many of these churches were subsidized from the general church level for more than a decade. The first one was in Hamilton, Ontario, Canada and each regional conference followed. I recall churches at McMinnville, Tennessee, Skyline View near Harrisburg, Pennsylvania, Ontario, California, Mountain View in Colorado Springs, Colorado, and Baltimore, Maryland.

By the time of my involvement in the early 1970's church leaders were changing to a new pattern. During these years one of the bishops was assigned the role of Director of Evangelism and Church Planting. It was a role I personally carried for some of those years.

Evangelism was always on the agenda of the quarterly meetings of the bishops. We would discern growth areas based on demographic studies and close to existing churches. We would seek people who would become involved in Bible studies, both from existing churches and new believers.

Then church leaders would encourage and challenge the gathering group of people to call a pastor and care for facilities.

There was some financial subsidy up front, usually for five years on a declining basis, with hopes the group would be on their own by the end of five years.

During the years from 1975 to 2000 we again had a surge of growth from 11,000 members to 24,000. It could be noted here that for years financial subsidy for church extension came by way of the General Conference Church Extension budget and for many years was part of the Board for World Missions. But in the mid-seventies dialogue with colleagues in the east led us to begin raising funds in the west with what we called "church growth dinners." These kinds of fund raising events have been part of the financial base of most Regional Conferences for church planting in the United States. The Canadian Conference functioned more with a unified budget.

There was some consensus among us to become God's people in contemporary culture by building on strong foundations but willing to change the ways we related to people. Thus there was an accent on our core values and at the same time a willingness to try new ways of evangelism.

Earlier, prior to the 1960's the Brethren in Christ had methods of outreach by way of Sunday Schools, Revivals and Camp Meetings.

Now there were new movements such as Evangelism Explosion, Campus Crusade's Four Spiritual Laws, and Fuller School of World Missions Church Growth Principles. In many ways we borrowed from all of these and more. There were numerous Bible Study programs that were also tools for Evangelism.

My involvement was blest by team workers who supported both vision and practice. Aaron and Martha Stern, Joyce and Glenn Ginder, Gordon and Eunice Engle were core group people who believed and gave themselves to church growth. I might mention Gordon and Eunice Engle sold their residence and moved to a new community to assist in a church planting. It was an example of what our earlier church preachers called, "selling out" and making a full commitment.

Lay leaders on regional boards believed we could do new plantings and they supported efforts with time, energy and money. Quarterly meetings with bishops and church leaders accented growth across the church and helped keep us unified as a people.

Reflection on 1972-1996 indicates these years were times of challenge and growth and we had several priorities.

First and foremost we remembered it was the Lord's church. I believe in prayer and would likely spend more time and energy in prayer if I had another opportunity like the one given during these years.

There were some pleasant surprises that the Lord gave us during these decades. The movement of Cubans to south Florida would eventually aid us in faster growth. The coming of other ethnic groups among us opened our eyes to new ways of evangelism. Our participation in the international Brethren in Christ Fellowship would enable us to learn from the churches overseas that had stronger growth patterns than we in North America.

With the reality of being human in a church with humanity, as well as the power of the Holy Spirit, it was apparent we needed VISION, PEOPLE and RESOURCES.

The VISION had to come from within. We had to believe in Jesus and in his people. As John Wimber reminded me, "you can always count on God, but watch out for some of his people." The vision we cast was to plant ten new churches in ten years in the Pacific Conference. I had to believe that in my head and heart and then boldly announce it to people and ask them to believe it.

Less ambitious goals were set in the Midwest Conference but there we also launched out into new areas. The best efforts were made in assigning pastors and moving into more populated areas. The Midwest churches were willing to support those efforts.

Some of the factors that led us to acceleration in church growth during the years of 1972-1984 included:

- a leadership mode that was willing to take risks
- believers involved in Bible Study and prayer groups
- pastors who sensed a call from God to plant churches with specific multi-year plans for growth
- believers willing to give themselves and finances to plant new churches
- training and screening of persons who were called to plant new churches

As for motivation, some of my personal beliefs moved me and the people who worked with me. Phrases I often used were: *"Church Growth is people." "The more pastors, congregations and people give of themselves and their resources, the more they will experience growth." "The longer a pastor and congregation work together the better it is for both." "The journey is the destination." "The process is the goal."* These concepts were shared often and repeatedly with pastors and church planting people.

As for PEOPLE: I believed in persons Jesus brought to us. Our existing churches and new churches would join me in that belief. I want to affirm the people in our churches in the Pacific and Midwest Conferences. These people took risks with me as a young leader that far exceeded my expectations. Sometimes their faith and trust scared me.

The other area of adventure with people was seeking new pastors. This was exciting with my colleagues and churches being open to bring new faces and names to our church family. Certainly we had some experienced persons true and tried, Wenger, Brubaker, Engle, Byer, Longenecker, Sider, etc. But when we added Feeney, Ernst, Ryan, Carter, Peabody, Finley, Goswiller, Morey, Negrete, White, etc., we were adding some non-ethnic people.

We were open to bring in pastors from other church families who had a passion and belief for growth. Bruxy Cavey, for example, led a new kind of model for growth in Toronto in the Canadian conference. Rod White has shown us a new model for the city of Philadelphia in the Atlantic Conference.

We did not have the screening processes in the earlier years, which I believe has been an improvement in calling church planting pastors. But basically, "Church is people" and growth will happen when people and pastors find a common vision and give it their best.

Some small churches and larger churches had differing gifts.

It is helpful to recognize growth that may be other than a church plant. The Mountain View church plant in Colorado Springs, Colorado sent at least four young pastors into the harvest. A number of our traditional churches have spawned several new church plantings by giving up people and finances.

I know, for example, the Midwest Zion church has sent at least six missionaries over the years. They were always good to their pastors and, more recently, helped by employing pastors they had evangelized who in turn started new churches. And Zion gave the church a bishop's wife. This wife I know has supported church growth. My wife, Marlene is the granddaughter of Bishop M. G. Engle who was one of our early holiness preachers that opened new paths for the Brethren in Christ.

Let me affirm my wife's faith, perception, intuition and grace. She often gave me support and wise correction, but most of all unwavering love and loyalty. Her strength at home and encouragement in my calling and training made possible my life in the church. She most certainly reared our children when I was absent, for many years about fifty percent of the time. I owe much to her love and companionship. So we should recognize different kinds of growth and encourage all. And at the same time we can and should hold each other accountable for the stewardship of resources.

As for RESOURCES, God gives each of us time, energy and money. If you have plenty of one you won't need as much of the other two, but it moves faster if you have more energy and money than time. Go figure. In the Pacific Conference in 1972, an annual regional conference church growth budget of several thousand dollars wouldn't cut it.

And as for energy, I believed Jesus wanted some new energetic leaders. So with some new believers and new pastors we launched a pattern of growth and it was an exciting time.

Did every one of our church plants become what we had hoped? No. I was hoping church plants would grow faster and start more new churches.

Did we see new growth and new life? Yes. Our first plant, Solid Ground in Alta Loma, California, is now one of our larger congregations in the Pacific Conference.

Did we see new people come to Jesus? Yes.

Did all the new churches survive? No. But would I do it again? Yes!

It is better to try something new beyond what you have done even if you fail, than to do nothing! It is better to heed the call of Jesus to make disciples and begin new cells of believers than just keep our existing churches feeding the well-nourished and satisfied believers.

I close with the motivating words of Jesus that were at the center of all our motivations and efforts.

> *"Therefore go and make disciples of all nations, baptizing them in the name of the Father and of the Son, and of the Holy Spirit, and teaching them to obey everything I have commanded you."*

Matthew 28

Acknowledgements

Special thanks to our daughter, Bernice Worley, who edited, formatted, and proof read the manuscript. She was most helpful in assisting me through the publishing phase of this book.

I am indebted to our two children, Bernice and Bruce, and their spouses, Robert and Carol, and to Bishop Perry Engle for reading the manuscript and offering good advice.